THE SUMMER OF THE WITCH

Maisie Raine was a teacher for almost 30 years, enjoying the involvement with young people. She is fascinated by local history and folklore and encouraged her students to use their imagination and ask questions about the world around them.

She lives in Durham, on a dairy farm on the top of a hill with partner Barry and dog Alfie. They overlook a beautiful valley, and a village very much like the magical "Dunchester"!

THE SUMMER OF THE WITCH

Maisie Raine

THE SUMMER OF THE WITCH

Olympia Publishers
London

www.olympiapublishers.com
OLYMPIA PAPERBACK EDITION

Copyright © Maisie Raine 2009

The right of Maisie Raine to be identified as author of
this work has been asserted in accordance with sections 77 and 78 of
the Copyright, Designs and Patents Act 1988.

All Rights Reserved

No reproduction, copy or transmission of this publication
may be made without written permission.
No paragraph of this publication may be reproduced,
copied or transmitted save with the written permission of the
publisher, or in accordance with the provisions
of the Copyright Act 1956 (as amended).

Any person who does any unauthorized act in relation to
this publication may be liable to criminal
prosecution and civil claims for damage.

A CIP catalogue record for this title is
available from the British Library.

ISBN: 978-1-905513-92-5

This is a work of fiction.
Names, characters, places and incidents originate from the writer's
imagination. Any resemblance to actual persons, living or dead, is
purely coincidental.

Illustrated by Sarah Austin

First Published in 2009

Olympia Publishers part of Ashwell Publishing Ltd
60 Cannon Street
London
EC4N 6NP

Printed in Great Britain

This book is for…

Everyone who enjoys a good story, and is fascinated by the world they know about – and the world they don't.

Especially for…

Barry, always my Rock, for Anne, sister and friend, and for Stephanie, who likes spooky tales.

It's also dedicated to the folk of "Crow Hill Farm" and the inhabitants of "Dunchester" – they know who they are!

Also for our family in Qormi, and for the two Alfies and Skips.

For kids and staff, past and present, of Oxclose Community School.

And remembering May, Bill, Mick, Molly and Wally.
With love.

BEFORE THE BEGINNING

He came out from the trees and looked across the valley, a small, slight figure, dressed in roughly fashioned furs and carrying a short wooden spear. He breathed in the air deeply and squatted on the ground. With the tip of his spear, he scratched away at the surface of the soil, crumbling it in his fingers. He laid his hand flat on the grass, listening intently for a long time. His eyes followed the path of birds and all around him was the rich, moist smell of the earth and the woods. All day he had observed and tested this place and at last he thought himself satisfied. He remained motionless for some time, becoming one with his surroundings, so still that a hare emerging from some long grass was surprised by his presence and took off suddenly down the hill. He watched this sacred animal, observing the pattern of its path, knowing that this too would tell him secrets about this place.

This would be a good place for his tribe. They had made the long journey from the north, driven by the colder weather and they needed to rest. They were waiting in the valley for him now, eager to hear his decision. And what would he tell them? That this was a rich, fertile land, with ample fruits and berries, fish and game. There was water and a good supply of wood, and no evidence of human habitation. It would be a safe home – and yet – he looked at the clouds, grey and low lying, almost touching the tops of the hills across the valley.

Yet there was something else, something he'd felt only once before on the long journey south. This was a place where the earth spirits were strong, where their world almost touched the world of men. He would cast what spells he knew, but then it would be up to the people who would come after him, to struggle and survive against the dark. He got to his feet and began to make his way back down the valley.

******

Over the centuries, this corner of the North East of England knew invaders and monsters, monks and saints. It was a land of mist and clouds, and strong, brave people. Battles were fought, as the fate of the land was decided, miracles occurred and finally the White Christ claimed victory over the ancient gods. But in the valley, and in the hills around, the earth spirits remained close, sometimes sleeping, but always present.

Chapter One

ABI ARRIVES

The journey from the station was as bad as she'd dreaded. Dad went on and on, as if he didn't want to leave any empty spaces between the words. He looked different, dressed in fashionable casual shirt and jeans, and he'd changed his hair style, but then it was three years since Abi had seen him. He pointed out the castle as they drove past, and the cathedral, looking as if they were growing out of the solid rock beneath them. Then came the university building where Christine worked, and the local radio station where Dad was a manager. Durham felt ancient, all grey stone and narrow, crooked streets.

Abi didn't say much, snuggled in the front passenger seat, staring out of the window. She caught a faint reflection of herself in the window – big eyes in a small face, long mousey hair. She thought that "mousey" was a good name for her. Always in new situations she felt lumpy and dull. She wished she was bright and bubbly, saying clever, funny things. Once again, she decided she hated being twelve-going-on-thirteen. As her grandma said, it was an "awkward age" – not a child anymore, and not yet ready to be a grown up.

She badly wanted her Dad to feel proud of her, to love her, but the dark thoughts remained in her mind. If she'd been different – looked different, said different things – would he have stayed with them? Was it she who had somehow caused the rows and the shouting? He chuntered on, not seeming to notice how quiet she was, asking about her school and her friends and Buster, her cat. He never mentioned Abi's mum. Abi wondered if grown ups sometimes felt as nervous as kids do – was that why he was talking so much and saying so little?

The new hospital at the edge of the city flashed by, and now they were driving through open country. Abi felt a wave of misery wash over her as she wondered how she would get through the next two weeks. How would she get through the next few minutes? It's a big thing to meet your Dad's live-in girlfriend.

They drove by fields full of fat, cartoon-like sheep and cows, and she glimpsed the isolated farmhouses, set back from the road. She wondered how people lived so far out of town. What did they do for entertainment? How would she spend the time stuck miles away from civilisation? Once again she wished she'd never come, but Mum was looking forward to her first proper holiday in years, and now that Dad was "settled" he wanted to spend time with her, and have her meet Christine.

Yet more fields and animals. A farm shop and "pick your own fruit" signs. How boring was this?

"Here's the village," Dad said, a little too brightly, and Abi saw a group of new detached houses, a 30mph speed notice and a board saying "Welcome to Dunchester".

"YOU'RE welcome to it," she muttered.

After the new buildings came the square stone houses of the original village, a church, a pub, a few shops. Again came the thought: this is the middle of nowhere. What'll I DO here for the next two weeks?

The car left the village to climb a steep hill where trees linked their branches in a thick, leafy arch over the road. Dad was saying what a lovely place this was, and describing the antics of their two cats, brothers George and Henry. Abi just wanted to tell him not to try so hard.

At the top of the hill, they turned into a narrow track, with fields on either side. She noticed a lonely, ancient tree next to a fence, side by side with a tall standing stone. Opposite was a sharp turn down a path covered on both sides by bushes – and there was the cottage. Christine had heard the car and had come out to greet them. She was small, with dark curly hair, and two black and white cats wound themselves around her ankles. She came towards Abi, who froze in panic. What would she say? God, would she have to kiss her? Christine solved the problem with a quick, easy hug, and Abi realised how sticky and hot she felt after the hours on the train.

A wash made her feel slightly better. They'd made the rented farm cottage cosy and welcoming, in the kind of designer country-style you see in Sunday magazines, Abi thought, determined to be picky about it. Hundreds of books were lined on shelves around the living room, and Abi was relieved to see a large TV set in the corner. That was something, at least – maybe there would even be a computer somewhere?

She hadn't realised how hungry she was, and she ate the roast chicken and vegetables with enjoyment. She concentrated on her meal, trying to ignore the conversation going on around her, full of private jokes and gossip about people known to Dad and Christine. Dad was relaxed and happy, and Abi recognised that this was his new life. Mum had a new life, too, going off to Greece with her friends. Abi felt that she was the only one not able to move on – the odd one out. She felt herself a stranger here, and had to blink hard as tears and tiredness hit her.

Dad was saying, "So, Abi, you'll have to amuse yourself during the next few days. Christine is preparing for this inspection at the university, and we're busy changing the computer set up at work – sorry about that. But the weather forecast is great and you'll be able to relax and get a tan in the garden. And we'll meet up with you after work, of course."

"I've asked the kids at the farm to come and meet you," added Christine. "I'm not sure when that'll be, but I know they'll be here. They're about your age."

Abi knew that the cottage was on farm land, and she certainly didn't want to meet those country kids. They were sure to be boring and uncool, but she made herself smile and nod. She had a bath and went to bed early, feeling tired out and a little bit weepy. She was glad to leave Dad and Christine to their red wine and TV. She heard them talking softly together and wondered if were they talking about her.

Her bedroom was small but comfy, with pale pastel walls and a cheerful, old-fashioned patchwork cover on the bed. Good – another TV sat on a table in the corner. At least she could spend her time here, watching telly. Then she didn't need to speak to anyone. She turned out the light and gazed out of the window.

Fields rolled down to where the village lay in a fold of land. It was almost dark, a soft, shadowy evening. Sheep were dotted around like cotton wool balls and a few birds chattered to each other as they settled to sleep. The first stars were coming out and Abi decided to leave her curtains open. If anyone was to ask her why, she'd never admit that it was because it was a nice view. Nice, but still boring. She slept soundly.

Abi, Stewart, Kate and Tom

Chapter Two

WELCOME TO DUNCHESTER!

Abi woke the next morning to bright sunshine. She blinked to find herself in this strange room, but then remembered where she was. Dad and Christine had gone off to work, and she felt as if she really was on holiday now, with the whole day spread in front of her, to do as she wanted. She forgot about her resolve of the night before, to stay in her room and watch TV. She was rested after a good night's sleep and she was eager to start her day. She washed, pulled on clean jeans and T-shirt, and went to find orange juice in the fridge and bread for the toaster. Then she opened the kitchen door to enjoy the fresh air. One of the cats (Henry?), sleeping on a bench, lazily opened one eye to look at her. Everything felt new and fresh, and the day was already hot.

She tuned into a music programme on the kitchen radio, singing along under her breath to the music as she prepared her breakfast. She remembered the magazines she'd brought for the train journey yesterday – she hadn't read two of them. Sitting outside in a shady place seemed like a very good idea.

Hunting around in the garden shed produced an old lounger which looked well worn and comfortable. She chose a spot in the front garden and soon she was settled with her magazines and another glass of juice. The sun grew hotter, a bee droned lazily by, and Abi sighed. This was so good; she felt all relaxed and sleepy – totally chilled. The magazine drooped in her hands. She thought she'd just close her eyes for a few minutes and enjoy a rest.

From a long way off, she heard whispers and laughing.

"Maybe she's dead – although I can hear snores."

She sat up quickly. "I'm not dead, I was only resting with my eyes shut. And I don't snore."

Three faces looked at her over the gate. They looked so alike that it was almost comical to see them together – frank, open faces and freckles, two boys and a girl, obviously related. The girl spoke.

"You're Abi."

"Yes."

"Christine asked us to come and meet you, so we're here."

Abi nodded. She was still annoyed at the rude remark about snoring, but thought she'd better be friendly and show them some politeness. Then they might just go away.

"Come in, then." But the three were already inside the garden, escorted by the biggest, hairiest dog Abi had ever seen.

Falling onto the grass, they introduced themselves as Kate, Tom and Stuart – and their dog was Alfie. Tom said he could just fancy a biscuit and went inside, obviously familiar with the layout of Christine's kitchen and returning with some chocolate cookies.

"He's a pig," Kate muttered. "No manners and hollow legs."

Abi thought it wasn't really on to go taking food from someone else's house, but thought it was best to keep that to herself. At least the three were easy to talk to. She forgot her usual shyness with strangers, and was soon joining in the conversation about home and schools. Kate was a year older than Tom and took her position very seriously. Tom liked sports and not much else, and Stuart, the youngest, was bright and was into horror stories – the ones he was allowed to read or watch on video. Kate obviously bossed the boys mercilessly, treating them like inferior beings, and they allowed her to do so, to keep the peace, Abi thought. Tom was told by his sister that three biscuits were enough, and they were now taking Abi to see the village.

They walked up the track, passing the farm buildings, and came to two stone houses, set side by side.

"The Old Farm House is where Nana and Grandad live, and we live in the New Farm House," Tom told her. "It's a bit grim up here in the winter, but Nan and Grandad can tell you stories about bad winters in the olden days that'd make your hair curl!"

"See that?" Stuart was pointing to a barn they were passing. "That was once a chapel. When there were a few more people living up here, the landowner wanted everyone to know how rich and good he was, so he built his own private chapel.

Cool, or what? You can tell by the shape of the windows, but we only use it for storing things now."

They told Alfie, "Stay", much to his disgust and went on down the footpath to the village. As they chattered on, Abi was surprised at how much they knew about trees and plants and wildlife, as well as about the people who had lived there in the past. Abi hated history at school, regarding it as a totally useless subject – why learn about a lot of dead people, anyway? But here was Kate, talking about Romans, Saxons and Vikings as if she knew them well. Their family had farmed this land for generations, and their love of the place came naturally.

The footpath eventually brought them into a small car park behind the main street. New houses had been built on the village outskirts, but this was the original Dunchester, a ribbon of honey-coloured stone houses and shops, sleepy and lazy on this sunny morning. Her new friends had proudly told her that "dun" was the ancient English word for "hill" or "high place" while "chester" came from the Roman word for "camp", referring to the base which had been built on the valley slopes to supply the soldiers manning Hadrian's Wall, further to the north.

"Let's have something to eat before we do anything," Tom suggested and led the way to a shop in front of which a sign stated 'Gift Shop. Coffee room upstairs. Please enter'.

Kate shook her head. "That boy will be twenty stone soon."

"Get away, I'm a growing lad, I need my food," her brother was now opening the door.

The shop was cool and dark, filled with the things you always find in country gift shops – boxes of fudge, fancy soap, colourful tea towels. A display stand of picture postcards stood to one side, and Abi glanced at them. Maybe she'd buy one as a memento of her stay. There was a good selection of views, but Abi was drawn to a sepia photograph of the main street, as it must have looked many years ago. In an oval sign in the centre of the card were printed the words 'Dunchester, the Witch Village'.

Abi felt strangely cold, and she shivered briefly.

"Witch Village?" she asked Kate. "Did witches live here?"

Kate followed her to the counter where she paid for the card. "Only one, as far as I know, Jane Wake."

She pointed to a collection of fridge magnets, all showing the same thing: a witch riding on a broomstick, with her tall pointed hat, black cloak, long sharp nose, and grinning in an evil way. The typical cartoon character from a thousand fairy tales.

The boys had already gone upstairs to the coffee shop and Tom had charmed the waitress into giving them the best table, set in the window and overlooking the street. They ordered cokes and a bacon sandwich for Tom.

"You are a pig," his sister told him.

"Yes, but I'm lovely," he answered modestly, with an angelic smile.

The café was busy at this time of day, with people meeting friends and resting after shopping. Tom passed the time by waving and grinning widely at some of the old ladies sitting at other tables. Their faces showed that they were desperately trying to think who he was, and many even returned his smile.

"Will you behave," hissed Kate. "One of these days you'll get into big bother!"

Then Tom made a mistake. A tall, smartly dressed woman entered, intent on finding an empty table. Tom's face creased into an enormous silly grin and he crossed his eyes to add to the effect. He gave her a huge wink before realising who she was.

"Good morning, Tom Oaken," she said grimly. "Still up to your silly tricks, I see?"

Tom collapsed into an embarrassed silence, his freckled face turning pink.

Stuart laughed slyly. "That's Miss Carson, Tom's teacher in primary school. He's still petrified of her."

The bacon sandwich arrived and Tom ate in silence, still a bit embarrassed. Abi sipped her coke and looked at the postcard she'd bought.

"So, who was this witch, Jane something?"

"Jane Wake," Kate told her. "She lived here hundreds of years ago and killed some children. She was actually burned on the village green, opposite the King's Head pub. Little kids are still threatened that if they're bad, Jane Wake will come and take them away."

"We sang a song about her when I was in infant school," Stuart remembered. "The Good Wife Jane."

Abi thought about this. "How come she was a witch and a Good Wife? What was the song?"

Stuart shrugged. "Can't remember. You're talking about years ago, you know, I was only about five." He sounded as if this had been centuries ago. Kate shook her head. "I really should know more about her, but you'll have to talk to Grandad Bill. He knows loads about local history and stuff."

They finished their drinks and went outside. The street was now bustling with morning shoppers. They crossed the road to the sturdy grey church, looking as if it had watched over the village forever. The churchyard was quiet and serene, full of ancient gravestones, many leaning over as if talking to each other. They pushed open the heavy wooden door and entered the church.

The door creaked to close behind them, and Abi looked around her. This was obviously a very aged building, calm and peaceful after the busy street. She could smell furniture polish, flowers and candles. There was something else there – she thought about the many generations of people who had met to pray there, in times of joy, or sickness, or war. They seemed to have left a bit of themselves behind, and this was a comforting feeling, that some things go on and on. A side door opened and a young man came in, carrying a book.

"Hi kids – thought it was you coming into the church, Tom. Your granddad was saying he'd been looking for this book and I saw it in the market at Durham. Will you give it to him?"

"Course I will," said Tom, taking it from him. "Paul, this is our friend Abi. She's staying here on holiday and we're showing her around. Paul's our vicar."

Abi thought he was a very unusual vicar. His long hair was pulled back into a ponytail, he wore denim jeans and shirt, and ancient trainers. They shook hands politely.

"What do you think of our St Michael's, then, Abi?" he asked. "Over five hundred years old and still standing strong."

"It's a lovely church," Abi replied. "I was thinking of all the people who must have prayed here over the years, whatever may have been happening in the world outside."

"Indeed," Paul Rose nodded. "And a lot of their descendants still live in the village today. Many families seem to have settled here for good. It's amazing that the same names crop up in our records, as folk are born and christened, marry, have a family and die. You're right – life goes on, no matter what!"

"Abi, come and see this," Stuart called softly.

He was standing in a bright patch of colour, as the sun filtered through a stained-glass window and made a rainbow of pattern on the stone floor.

The picture on the window showed a very tall, thin woman, with long flowing dark hair. She looked fierce and frightening. The woman was tied to a wooden post and a crowd of people looked on as a man stacked branches around her. A ribbon came from her mouth as if to carry her words, and Abi struggled to read the old-fashioned letters. "Forever" – what did that mean?

"Is it a prayer?"

Paul Rose shook his head.

"Hardly. That's out local witch, Jane Wake. She was burned just opposite the church, and her final words were to curse the village 'forever'."

Abi felt a coldness throughout her body and couldn't decide if this was because of the stone walls around her, or the thought of a curse laid on an entire village "forever".

In the village shop, Abi finds postcards of "Dunchester, The Witch Village".

Chapter Three

HISTORY RULES!

They decided that it was really too hot to do anything except to chill out in the shade with a cool drink.

As they walked back from the village, Kate suddenly said, "Let's go and visit Jonty."

Stuart nudged his sister.

"Bet Abi will be dead impressed with his Jag."

Abi wondered at their fit of laughter.

On the rise out of the village, a small stone-built house was set back from the road, with a track leading up to it. A terrier came bouncing excitedly towards them.

"Hello Bodger."

Stuart bent down to stroke him.

Behind the house was an incredible collection of ancient domestic objects. Armchairs, tables, pots and pans were all heaped together as if they were exotic plants growing out of the grass.

"Graveyard for old things," Tom murmured to Abi. "Guess what's in the barn over there?"

"More old things?" guessed Abi, and Tom nodded.

"Jonty always lives in hope that one day he'll find something really special. He collects all kinds of things, and get rid of nothing."

Outside the back door, a kind of wooden trolley had been supplied with two long arms and attached to an old three-wheel cycle. The trolley was painted in gaudy colours, with the words 'J. GINKS SCRAP MERCHANT' picked out in uneven red letters on the side. This, Abi guessed, was "Jonty's Jag".

Out of the house came a tall, thin man, balding, but with a narrow crown of hair which decorated his head like a wreath.

"Hello. What you's up to, then?"

They exchanged comments about the hot weather, and Tom asked Jonty if he had come across anything interesting lately. A sly look came over Jonty's face, and he tapped the side of his nose.

"I've heard there's a sale at Moresby Hall next week. Should be some good stuff there!"

Tom spun some complicated tales, each more unlikely than the last, about items picked up for pence at car boot sales and proving to be valuable antiques. Jonty listened, nodding his head and rubbing his hands.

"Aye, only a matter of time afore I'm lucky and I find something special!"

On the way home, they discussed his hopes. Poor Jonty, always living in dreams of being lucky one day! They reached the Old Farm House at last. A man sat in the shade, and Abi was introduced to Grandad Bill. They all pulled up garden chairs to his table, on which a huge mug of tea stood in front of him. Tom gave him the book from Paul Rose, and Bill took it, nodding his thanks.

"We've been telling Abi about this place," Kate told him. "We said she'd best talk to you about some of the history."

Abi thought that Bill Oaken looked just like all the farmers she'd ever seen in pictures, red face, stout, and with sharp, friendly eyes. Even in this heat, he wore a cap. She liked him right away. Tom went in search of cold drinks and sandwiches from the house, returning soon with supplies sent out by Nana.

"What do you want to know, Abi?" Bill asked. "We've a whole lot of history here, if you're interested."

Although Abi had never been much interested in long ago happenings, she settled down to listen to the old farmer. He'd make a cool history teacher, she thought – much better than old "Sell by" Selby back at school.

Bill Oaken loved the land which his family had farmed for centuries. His son, Young Bill, father of Tom, Kate and Stuart, urged him to retire, yet he showed no desire to do so, and plainly he was a keen historian, with a deep feeling for the place in which he lived. He talked passionately about the people of the past, their lifestyles and beliefs, as if he'd known them personally. Then he went to fetch a little wooden box from the house, and opened it to show a delicate silver brooch worked with intricate whirls and loops.

It had been turned up in a field when a drainage ditch had been dug, and Bill believed it to be Viking work. Abi stroked it gently. This was the oldest thing she'd ever held in her hand.

"Someone must have loved this."

"Of course," said Bill. "People in the past had the same feelings and emotions as we have, and I'm sure someone was proud to own this."

Abi felt a sharp, achy feeling. These people were not just names in a book; they had lived and breathed, loved and hurt, they had had their worries and hopes. She remembered to ask about Jane Wake.

"Little Jane Wake," said Bill softly.

"LITTLE? She looked pretty big and scary in the church window," Stuart laughed.

"That window was made hundreds of years after she lived," Bill told him. "No one would have remembered what she'd looked like."

Abi remembered the witch fridge magnets she'd seen for sale in the shop and described them to Bill.

"Well, there again, I wouldn't call them reliable descriptions of what Jane looked like. They were made for only one reason."

"To get money out of tourists," Tom nudged Abi and laughed at her.

Bill nodded his agreement.

"All the cards and the souvenirs were made for commercial reasons, to make money – and to fit in with the ideas people have about witches. Jane probably couldn't read or write, so all we know about her comes from other people, and many of them would be against her, anyway."

Abi thought about this.

"But that's the only way we learn about history – things are written down by people who were there and we read about them today."

Bill shook his head.

"We have to be careful, Abi, and things in books can't always be trusted. In history, you need evidence – something you can check and trust. History was usually written by the educated powerful people, we rarely hear from the ordinary folk, especially not women, we only hear what other people say about them."

He took another drink of his tea.

"Everyone has their own point of view, and their own reasons for saying things, so we get their versions of events. Even eyewitnesses may have seen different things, or interpreted events in different ways – put their own slant or spin on things, like."

"So why do you say 'little' Jane Wake – what proof do you have that she was small?" Abi asked.

"She must have been – her shoes are still kept in the King's Head. She stood trial there. She was kept a prisoner in the cellar and burned outside on the green. Her shoes are tiny; she must have had small, slender feet – a little lass. I started making notes to write a book about the history of Dunchester, but never got it finished. I became interested in the story of Jane, but I never got around to writing it. I'll tell you more about her another time!"

"Do you believe there really were witches, Grandad?" Kate asked, helping herself to another sandwich.

"You believe in ghosts, but, don't you?" Stuart added eagerly.

Bill laughed and held up his hands.

"Hey, one at a time, please! Kate, I don't believe in pacts with the devil or things like that, but it does seem that some of these women in the past may have possessed some knowledge and skills which have been lost to us. They could heal people, and animals, and they knew a lot about the weather and the world around them. Maybe they knew about some kind of natural earth magic. And yes, "Stu Pot", I reckon I believe in ghosts – whatever they might be. I've seen some strange shadows and shapes around this place, and there's one little chap, dressed in furs and carrying a spear, comes round now and then. He looks over that gate, clear as clear can be. I'm never frightened, I like to think he's some kind of guardian of the place, keeping an eye on us and making sure we're all right."

"You often say this is a strange place, and things happen here," Kate said softly.

"I've seen and heard some odd things in my time," Bill spoke, as if to himself. "But then, a lot of folk around here have."

He shifted in his chair and drained the last of his tea.

"Some try to explain it by saying that we're close to the spirit world here – or that there may be some geological fault deep underground. Others blame electricity or some kind of magnetism in the earth. There are several ley lines crossing here – they're said to be ancient lines of power. Who knows? But I think that's enough mysteries for now – you'll all be having nightmares!"

Abi badly wanted to know more about all these things, but Grandad Bill was picking up his mug and preparing to go for his meal, so she made her way down the track. Back home, she found the salad things Christine had left in the fridge and began mixing them together. She'd made some new friends and she looked forward to seeing them the next day. And all those things that Old Bill had spoken about, earth magic and the rules of history – and what exactly were ley lines, anyway? She thought about Jane Wake and what her true story might be. So history was like a detective story – you had to look for facts and then test the evidence you found. She liked that idea.

She was chatty over the evening meal, and David and Christine were pleased that she'd enjoyed the day. She decided to keep some things to herself – she didn't want them to think that she was developing weird interests! Dad was a scientist and she guessed what he'd have to say about ley lines and ancient earth mysteries. He'd have some logical explanation for any odd thing which happened here. After the meal, she couldn't stop yawning and decided to have an early night.

From her bedroom window, she looked across the valley, where the first lights were appearing in some of the isolated houses. She thought about all the other people who had stood on this hill and looked at the same view. That's what history was all about – about people, real living people, not just long lists of kings and queens and battles. And it certainly wasn't as boring – or as simple – as she'd thought. Her last thoughts were about Buster, safe in the cattery back at home.

Joan was only a little lass – burned, she was – as a witch.

Chapter Four

JONTY FINDS 'SOMETHING SPECIAL'

Abi woke to another glorious summer day. She showered, dressed and ate a hurried breakfast. She was meeting the others that morning, but she would have the afternoon to herself as they were visiting an old aunt with their mother. She had already decided how she was going to use the time.

The two cats were napping again – this time, under a large bush outside the kitchen door. Abi thought it must be very pleasant to be a cat who was well cared for: not much to do, just eat and sleep in the sun. Not a bad life!

She thought she could hear some kind of motor outside, and voices, and she went to the front gate to investigate. Opposite, through the wooden fence, was the great standing stone, and the ancient tree, which now had a heavy chain fastened around it. The other end of the chain was attached to a tractor, being driven slowly forward by a small, balding man dressed in cap and overalls. Kate, Stuart and Tom, with a group of onlookers, were watching with interest. Kate grinned at Abi as she joined them.

"Frank said Dad told him to get rid of the tree. It's showing signs of disease. We're just waiting for Grandad to appear, he's always taken good care of that old tree – says it's special. He'll need a chill pill when he sees this!"

The tractor shunted painfully forward, and there came a great groan from the tree. It started to move slowly, a few inches at a time. Another tug from the tractor and the tree came up from the ground, its great roots bringing up a huge shower of earth.

The noise of the falling giant shook the ground underfoot, and Abi was saddened at the death of such an enormous living thing. She blinked. Just for a second, she thought she'd glimpsed something caught up in the roots, and then slipping back into the hole.

An angry shout came from the track. Jonty Ginks, one of the onlookers, grinned in expectation.

"You're in trouble now, Frankie boy – here's Old Boss!"

"Oh hell!" muttered Frankie. "Here we go."

Grandad Bill came storming towards them, face red with rage and waving a walking stick.

"Frankie! What do you think you're doing? Who told you to pull up that tree?"

"Hey, steady on, Boss," Frank Tate tried to calm the old man. "Young Boss told me to get rid of it. Said it's showing signs of disease and it was best to pull it."

"I'm not retired yet, Frank, just remember that – I'm still the Boss and I tell you what I want doing. Just you leave that now and come and see that fool son of mine. Thinks he knows everything. He'll have done some damage this time."

Old Bill was in a full blown rage, and everyone kept quiet.

Bill and Frank Tate, followed by the grinning crowd, made their way to the New Farm House. To the disappointment of the group, the door was slammed behind them and only faint raised voices could be heard from within.

"This happens more and more often now," Tom explained. "Grandad can't let go, and Dad can't wait to be in full charge. Sometimes it's hard for both of them."

The raised voices inside the house eventually calmed down, and sensing that the excitement was over, the little group dispersed to their own business. No one wanted to be around when Old Bill emerged.

Tom and the others walked back down the track and climbed through a gap in the fence to take a closer look at the felled tree. It looked sad and defeated lying on the ground and they gathered around it.

"This stone is ancient." Kate stroked her hand across its surface. "There's the remains of a stone circle up on Maiden Hill, and Grandad thinks it might have been brought down from there years ago."

"And the tree must have stood here for years," Stuart pointed at the massive thick, twisted roots. "Look how thick these are."

Abi remembered that she'd thought she'd seen something caught up in the woven tentacles as they were forced from the ground. She went to the side of the crater and peered down into the hole. No sign of anything. She must have imagined it.

"Come on," she said. "Let's go for a walk. Let's climb to the top of Maiden Hill. I'd like to see the stones there, and I bet you get great views from up the top."

******

When everyone had followed Grandad Bill and Frankie Tate, expecting to witness a huge row, Jonty had stepped through the gap in the fence.

Years of waiting for "something special" to happen had made his eyes sharp, and he had seen the grey shape caught up in the maze of roots, and then fall back into the hole. He gazed down into the pit – yes! – there was definitely something there. Something oblong and grey – a treasure chest! He scrambled down the side of the great hole, and just managed to lift the object, balancing on some of the exposed roots. He struggled to get it onto the ground – God, it was heavy! – and then lifted it onto his cart, covering it with some old sacks. Didn't want any prying eyes seeing what was his business!

Jonty couldn't wait to investigate his find. Reaching home, he pulled out some old newspapers from a pile in the corner of his kitchen and spread them out on the table. He carefully placed his treasure on them. He saw that it was a stone box, with a close fitting lid. He didn't like the skeletons carved on its top and sides, waving scythes and hourglasses – how creepy was that? Never mind that, he thought excitedly, let's see what was inside!

Bodger suddenly whined, put his ears back, and slunk into a corner, but Jonty was too busy examining the box to notice.

The lid was secured firmly, not budging as Jonty tugged and pulled at it. He brought a hammer and chisel from his toolbox and carefully attacked the join where the lid met the box. This could be really valuable, and he wanted to mark it as little as possible.

Finally, the chisel did its work, and the lid began to move. One last tap, and Jonty was able to remove it completely. He looked eagerly inside, and felt a bitter disappointment. This, then, was his "treasure" – not the coins or jewels he had imagined, but a few scraps of old cloth, something that looked like ashes – and were those things bits of bone? Yuk!

A sudden cold breeze touched his neck, causing the contents of the box to rustle slightly. Jonty looked around – had he left the door open? No, he'd thought not. He pursed his lips as he stared at the object on his table. Maybe he could take it to that Christine and ask her if the university might want to buy it. But then they'd ask to know how he'd come to have it and there'd be awkward questions to answer. No, not a good idea. He might put it in a boot sale as a planter for someone's posh garden, unless those spooky skeletons dancing around it put people off.

Jonty did as he usually did. He decided to put it to one side until he could get round to giving it a good clean and then decide how he could make the best profit from it. He opened the back door and Bodger shot out of the house, tail between his legs. Placing the stone box by the door, he stood the lid up by the wall. Then Jonty forgot about his latest discovery and thought he'd like a cup of tea. After that, he'd go down to the village and see what was going on there.

Chapter Five

ABI PLAYS DETECTIVE

Abi knew exactly how she would spend her afternoon. After making a quick sandwich, and eating it in the garden, she took to the footpath to the village. She passed Alfie, as usual suffering in the heat and lying in some shade, he lifted his head and half-heartedly wagged his tail as she passed. She thought about what Grandad Bill had told her, that in researching history you had to look for "evidence" and examine and test it to try to reach the truth about what had happened in the past.

She started her investigation in the little gift shop in the village. The bell above the door "pinged" as she entered, but the man at the counter didn't raise his head from the newspaper he was reading. The display about witches drew her. She noticed that there were three different kinds of postcards, all with local views, and all calling Dunchester "the witch village". Fridge magnets showed the witch of legend and fairy tale. Abi decided that none of these things told you anything about Jane Wake. Someone had heard that a witch had supposedly lived there and thought they'd make a profit out of visitors. She could learn nothing about Jane Wake here!

Her next stop was the public library. Once again, no one questioned her. The two girls behind the desk were busy attending to customers. Abi passed through the small wooden gate and found the section of books on local history and folklore. After looking carefully, she chose two books which looked promising and took them to a nearby table where she could read them.

One she could forget about right away; Jane Wake was mentioned just once, in a chapter describing religion and beliefs in seventeenth century North East England. The other book was much more relevant. In a chapter called "Witch Trials of the North East", Abi found Jane. She lived in the seventeenth century, and had been a well liked and respected member of the village community. She attended church and was a skilful healer of both humans and animals. People believed she could influence the weather and consulted her about many aspects of their everyday lives. She'd been taught her skills by her grandmother and she had a young daughter, although there was no mention of a husband. Jane always said that her skills came from a knowledge of nature and a good common sense. She denied any loyalty to the devil, claiming that she'd never use her skills to harm anyone.

In the summer of 1650, sweating sickness attacked the village. Jane nursed the sick, saving several lives and then took eight of the children away to a remote farmhouse where they stayed until the sickness died away. On their return to the village, Jane was greeted with gratitude and was celebrated as an accomplished healer and wise woman. Then, just five years later, a commission from Parliament came to Durham, to investigate the religious and political loyalties of the local population. Jane was denounced as a witch, there was a swift trial and she was found guilty. She was burned on the village green in June 1655. Jane never said a word in her own defence.

I'm not surprised about that, thought Abi. Poor Jane, she spent her life in the village, doing nothing but good. She'd never believe her own people would turn against her. I wonder what happened. She was a local heroine, saving those children, then someone denounced her as a witch. Maybe the story about Jane killing children got mixed up with her saving them. Maybe someone wanted to blacken her name. There's something wrong here – bits of the story are missing.

The evidence there in front of her seemed quite reliable. There were actual dates, and no obvious bias in the writing. Notes at the bottom of the page told the reader where the author had found his information – mainly in volumes of local records which you'd think would be quite dependable. From the notes, she found out that witchcraft had been a capital offence since 1563. Thoughtfully, Abi returned the books to the shelves and went back out into the sunlight.

She next visited the church, and spent some time in front of the stained-glass widow. She noticed how tall the artist had made Jane, and how frightening she looked, with a fierce expression, sharp features, and long black hair streaming behind her. Maybe this was done to make Jane look as threatening as possible, so that the people who had put her on trial would look brave and virtuous in defeating her.

"I'm getting to be good at this," Abi told herself, realising that she was enjoying the detective work.

Abi's last stop was at the "King's Head". A girl was collecting empty glasses from the wooden tables outside the pub, and Abi asked politely if she could see Jane Wake's shoes. The girl was friendly and Abi was directed down a stone passage way, hearing low voices from the bar on her right, and then great hoots of laughter. She had been told that she needed to go to the end of the passage and then take a door to her left. She entered a large room with a low ceiling probably a function room, hired out for parties, as it was empty of furniture. She found a light switch by the door and when the light flooded on, Abi saw a glass case on the wall opposite.

A small light within the case shone downwards, and a printed card underneath said that a local woman, Jane Wake, had been tried as a witch, and condemned to death by burning in the summer of 1655. The trial, held before government officials, had taken place in that very room, and Jane had worn those shoes. Bill was right: the shoes were tiny, like modern day ballerina-style slippers, made of soft black leather and tied with straps around the ankles.

Abi felt a sharp stab of pity. The living Jane had stood trial in this room, and this was all that was left of the woman. She was never able to describe or explain what happened next. It seemed that, in the space between two heartbeats, she was in that room, but in another time. She felt terror, her breath coming in great sobs as she pushed her way through the crowd, desperate to get to the front. Her cap had come off and she rubbed tears from her eyes with her sleeve. This was no dream. She could feel the press of people around her, she could smell tobacco smoke and stale beer, and she could hear the echo of voices from along way off. Then strong arms lifted her above the crowd, she heard a distant voice saying "no place for a bairn" and then she was carried from the room, struggling wildly to get free.

Now she was able to see the three men at the front of the room. Dressed in severe black and white, tall hats were placed on the table in from of them. Their faces were stern and they looked at her with clear dislike and mistrust. A small woman faced them, seated in a high-backed chair, dressed in a long dark dress of some rough material. Her hair was pinned up under a neat white cap and her eyes were huge in a pale face. The woman gave her such a look of love and compassion that Abi felt its force like a blow to her stomach.

Chapter Six

THE DEVIL'S OWN

Abi left the pub in a daze, not hearing the bargirl's cheery "Bye". She walked slowly home, totally drained of any feeling. Her chest felt tight and she found it hard to breathe. What had happened back there? There was no explanation. Maybe she was going mad. She'd better be careful that she didn't become obsessed with Jane Wake, that woman who had died on a summer day centuries ago. Her brain must be in overload or something. Best to lay off for a time, forget all about witchcraft and earth forces and whatever. Just do normal things and chill. She swallowed hard and felt sick.

Yet when she got home, she found herself hunting through Christine's large collection of books. Christine worked in the research unit of Durham University's History Department, and the walls of her cosy lounge were covered with shelves full of neatly stacked books and magazines.

She found a book about superstitious beliefs in Tudor and Stuart times, helped herself to an apple and a glass of chilled water, and settled herself at the table outside the kitchen. The book covered the sixteenth and seventeenth centuries, when the fear and dread of witchcraft had taken the lives of thousands of men, women and even children. It was enough for someone, out of spite or jealousy to accuse a neighbour of sorcery, and terrible consequences followed.

So called "witches" were tested and "walked" for hours, with a rope tied around their waist so they could be pulled up if they faltered. Exhausted and terrified, without rest, food or water, they would admit to any charges directed at them. They were searched and pricked with needles to seek out the marks supposedly put on their body when the devil had first claimed them as his own.

They were beaten and "swum" to see if water rejected them because of their sins, or, as in Jane's case, verbal testimony of witchcraft given by a respected member of the community was enough. Then, they were hanged or burned, all in the name of God. Some 200,000 supposed witches were tortured, burned, or hanged in Western Europe.

At the front of the book, there was a dedication, given as a sixteenth century anonymous inscription. As Abi read it, she felt a lump come to her throat.

> *"For those who were pricked, racked, and broken on the wheel for the sins of their inquisitors.*
> *For all those whose beauty stirred their torturers to fury, and for those whose ugliness did the same.*
> *For all those who were neither ugly nor beautiful, but only women who would not submit.*
> *For all those quick fingers, broken in the vice.*
> *For all those midwives, killed merely for the sin of delivering men into a imperfect world.*
> *For all those witch-women, my sisters, who breathed freer as the flames took them, knowing that death alone would cleanse them of the sin for which they died – the sin of being born a woman."*

So deep in her thoughts, Abi hadn't heard Christine come out of the house.

"Hello," she said, sitting down opposite Abi. "I managed to finish work a bit early. Fancy something to eat or drink?" She looked at Abi's book. "Ooh, heavy stuff, the witch trials!"

"I got interested in Jane Wake and I thought this might help me understand what was happening at the time." Abi explained. "This is shocking. How could people do such horrible things?"

"Superstition – strong – and wrong beliefs," mused Christine. "These women were uneducated, they had no power, no political pressure, and they were at the mercy of powerful, educated men. You know, some women confessed to witchcraft willingly, without being tortured? Maybe they really did believe they had been given dark powers – or they were made to believe it. Maybe they enjoyed their moment of fame and importance, the only one they'd ever known."

Abi shuddered. "What about Jane Wake?"

"I grew up in Dunchester, and I heard the stories about Jane when I was little. Many stories were legends, or scary ones made up for kids. I've always felt Jane was badly treated by history – just another woman made into a villain because she couldn't speak for herself."

"So you don't believe she was an actual witch?"

"I think she was a wise woman, skilled in healing and perhaps even possessing some ancient knowledge about the natural world – knowledge that was never written down and has been long forgotten."

"Strange things do happen in the valley, don't they?" Abi asked.

Christine laughed.

"You've been listening to Grandad Bill. But yes, there are loads of old stories and customs that people still follow here. The old folk especially will whisper that they've felt "presences" and maybe the experts might say that there's a lot of "psychic activity" in the area. We often have problems with the electricity supply, you know, and our watches and clocks sometimes stop, or act up. Folk talk about magnetism in the rocks – maybe it's the influence of ley lines. Maybe it's just that this is a remote village with its roots deep in the ancient past and is finding it hard to move into the twenty-first century!"

Christine moved to get up to return to the house.

"Still – one thing bugs me about Jane – really makes me think." She picked up Abi's glass.

"Jane was tried before three representatives of Parliament. Now, what on earth were they doing here, in a tiny place like Dunchester was at that time? They were the VIPs of their day. Now THAT'S a mystery!"

Abi returned to her book. She read that fear of a witch lasted even after death, and it was believed that a witch would only rest safely in her grave if she was buried "under wood and under stone". Something bothered her about that. She slowly closed the book and put it down. On a post opposite, a huge crow looked at her and cawed softly.

Chapter Seven

THE NIGHTMARE BEGINS

Next day, the heat was unbearable, even at nine in the morning. A blazing sun hit the earth like a hammer blow, as Abi set off to meet the others. She wondered what they would do today – not much, she hoped – much too hot. Being lazy and staying in the shade would be nice. She wasn't sure how much she would tell them about the events of yesterday. They had been too weird – and too personal – to share with other people. Her thoughts were interrupted by the sight of her friends, Grandad Bill and his son, standing in the field with a man dressed in jeans, T-shirt and Wellingtons.

Kate raised her hand in greeting as she approached, but one look at the faces in front of her was enough for Abi to see that something bad had happened here.

"What's happening?" she asked.

Tom's open, freckled face was tight with emotion.

"Twenty sheep," he said, his voice breaking, then repeating himself as if he couldn't believe what he was saying. "Twenty sheep, all killed last night. They'd had their blood drained from their bodies."

Abi now realised why canvas screens had been erected across a corner of the field.

The strange man – the local vet, Abi guessed – now answered a call on his mobile. Then he looked up, his face white and set.

"There's another twelve sheep dead the same way at Colin Horn's place, and more animals up at Highfield Farm," he told them.

A couple of farm workers had joined the little group, and muttered angrily. Country folk knew how hard and cruel nature could be, but this was something new and disturbing – fine animals killed for no reason, and in no way they recognised.

With a few last words to Young and Old Bill, and obviously concerned about the strange animal deaths, the vet drove off in his van. The small knot of people dispersed and the four friends looked at each other.

"What on earth happened here?" Abi asked. "Has anyone got any ideas at all?"

Kate blew out her breath loudly.

"Dunno – it happened in the night, but the farm dogs didn't bark. Something came, drew off the blood through their necks, and there's no sign of what did it."

"No one's seen anything like it," Tom went on. "No animal ever did anything like that."

"It could be zombies – or aliens, taking the blood of animals so that they can analyse it," suggested Stuart, who seemed to be the only one to be enjoying the situation.

Nobody could be bothered to tell him to shut up.

They decided to walk up to Highfield Farm to find out what exactly had happened there. The farm was a favourite destination for the local primary schools. Besides having the usual farm animals such as cows, sheep and goats, there were more exotic beasts – llamas, reindeer, and even a camel. Children were encouraged to play with and feed many of them, and small animals were even taken into schools for the children to become familiar with.

The walk took ten minutes, and nothing was said by anyone on the way. Kate dreaded to think what news would greet them when they reached the farm. They found the gates closed and a police car and van were parked on the grass verge. A police officer was on duty.

"Sorry kids, farm's closed today," he told them.

"Yes, we heard about the animals," Tom nodded. "We're from Crow Hill Farm and a lot of our sheep were killed last night. Have the police found anything out here?"

The policeman shook his head.

"Hard to say – the vet's here now. I heard that cows and sheep were dead, and a donkey. To be honest, security's poor here; there's easy entry. The owners planned to put up security cameras at the end of the season, but it's a doddle to get in now."

There was nothing else to see or to find out, so they walked back again silently. The senseless death of so many animals, and the horrible way they had been killed had shocked and saddened them all. As they passed Jonty's house, Tom idly noticed that his door and windows were all closed, and the curtains drawn. A small bit of Tom's mind told him that this was unusual.

******

Jonty had settled down in his kitchen early that morning to read yesterday's paper. He opened the door to try to get a cooling breeze into the house, but it was little use. Suddenly, Bodger leapt up from where he had been lying under the table, whimpered, and raced out through the open door.

"Silly lump," Jonty muttered and went back to the sports pages.

Sunderland still had not made any signings, he saw. So much for the promised strengthening of the team for next season.

Deep in his reading, Jonty only vaguely felt a light current of air brush the back of his neck, as if someone had entered the kitchen and passed by him. He turned his head to look, but found he couldn't move any part of his body. His chest was unbearably tight and he felt as if an icy hand had gripped his spine. Every breath he took was agony. He could feel the hairs on the back of his neck rise in terror. What the hell was happening to him? He wondered in panic. Was this a heart attack? Was he about to die? Then, he lost awareness of anything around him, and felt he was in a deep pit, lost and solitary. He heard the voice deep inside his head.

"Listen and hear me, Master Jonty," it said, quiet but insistent, soft but strong. "I have need of you. You will help me and you will do all that I ask. You are my creature. I will not harm you but you must heed me for I have much work to do here."

Jonty found that he could nod his head in agreement.

At last he had found his "something special".

******

That night, Tom lay in a deep sleep. In the kitchen below his room, a fire had started. Slowly, Tom became aware of the acrid smell of smoke seeping up between the floorboards under his bed. Urgently, his mind told his body that he must wake up. But he found it impossible to move, and he hovered between sleep and waking in an increasing state of panic. No part of his body would obey his mental orders. He felt a growing heat all around, and could hear the sharp crackle of hungry flames. Just move one arm – try – try your hardest. You have to move to save yourself. He started to cough as his lungs filled with smoke. A scream began to form in his throat but came out of his mouth as only a weak croak. He forced his eyes open. With his utmost effort, he pulled himself up into a sitting position, sweating and gasping for breath. He looked around frantically – everything was normal, just as it should be. No fire. No smoke. No danger. He sat on the edge of his bed, blinking and breathing deeply.

******

Abi couldn't move her arms. They were tied tightly behind her back, tied to a wooden post. She was set above the heads of the crowd, looking down on them. She could see their faces, the faces of her friends and neighbours, showing – what? Shock? Horror? Compassion? A man stepped forward, carrying a blazing bundle of twigs and thrust it into the wood placed around her feet. Then this was the end – would no one stop it? Would no one speak out? She coughed as the smoke reached her throat, and tried desperately to pull against her bonds. Her eyes prickled in the rising smoke, but she tried to keep them open; she was too afraid to close them and accept death. She must keep a firm grip on life for as long as she could.

A farmer she knew held up a little girl to her, as usual she had lost her cap and her nut brown hair shone in the summer sun. The child was crying huge, gasping sobs and she held out her arms to the person she loved most in the world. She hadn't wanted the child to be there, yet it was a last kindness. If only the farmer would take her away now, so that she saw no more. Yes, he was turning now, making his way through the silent crowd, the child perched on his shoulders, although she still desperately turned her head to see. No one would speak out for her now. They were all afraid of the three men from Parliament, standing grimly at the edge of the crowd, sombre in their black suits and tall hats. She lost consciousness, her last feelings being fear, betrayal, abandonment. And a deep and everlasting desire for revenge.

Abi woke up, her throat raw from sobbing as if her heart would break.

******

Helen Carson had complained, time and time again, about the ancient electrical wiring in her classroom. Time and again the school governors assured her that there was definitely no danger, and that a full rewiring programme would be carried out as soon as the school budget would allow. Yet here she was, with twenty Year Six children, huddled in a corner, seeing the wall of fire roaring closer and closer. The fire alarm was shrieking shrilly, even above the frightened screaming of her pupils, clinging to her and trusting her to save them.

She tried to reassure the students, but she was rapidly losing all hope of rescue. The flames were between them and the doorway into the hall and the high old-fashioned windows were way above their heads and impossible to reach. The crackle of flames and the intense heat were worsening by the minute and she felt herself drifting away, to a remote place deep within herself. Was this how it was to die? Her mouth opened in a scream, and she sat up rigid in her own bed. Shock, horror and relief washed over her in great waves.

******

He knew he shouldn't have brought the child, but she'd begged to see her mother, and a part of him wanted to do at least this for Jane. He wished he could do a lot more, and knew that many others felt the same, but none dared speak out in case they were named as friends of the witch. That little Jane didn't deserve to die, she had done so much good, but now here she was, close to death. He held up the child to her mother. The crowd was silent – there'd be many a troubled mind that night, he reckoned –

including his own. Now the fire was well away, the sound of crackling wood sharp and angry as the spiteful flames reached for the woman. The child must see no more. He felt her turning and reaching back, heard her frightened screams. He hurried away as fast as he could.

******

Old Bill started, suddenly waking, and lay gasping. What a terrible, fearful dream – more like a vivid memory, lost in time. He struggled to try to understand what might be happening.

******

In the morning, as friend greeted friend in Dunchester, the intense and terrifying dreams of the night were shared and discussed. All were different in their detail, but all involving fire and death.

Chapter Eight

TOM'S DEN

Abi turned on the local TV news as she made coffee and toast. It had been far too hot to sleep properly last night, and that horrible dream had upset her more than she cared to admit to herself. Why had she dreamed like that? Yet it hadn't felt like a dream – she'd felt like she'd actually been there, a feeling just as real as she'd experienced in the pub. She must be going mad – or becoming obsessed by Jane Wake. She had to get her mind away from the woman who had lived three hundred and fifty years ago.

Someone was being interviewed on TV, and a flash at the bottom of the screen identified him as a fruit farmer from Dunchester. Abi turned up the sound. He was saying that in thirty years of farming in the area, he had never known such high temperatures, especially over the last two days. He was in danger of losing his entire crop, and all his colleagues in the locality were also in trouble. Back in the studio, a friendly presenter smiled widely and calmly reported that unfortunately, the forecast was for another extremely hot and sunny day, with the highest temperature centred around Dunchester.

"So lets enjoy the lovely weather – except if you're a Dunchester fruit farmer," he ended, with a cheeky wink.

******

Tom's pride and joy was his "den", an ancient caravan used for tea breaks by a group of workmen who had done some work at the dairy a year ago. Tom had claimed the abandoned caravan when they left, and had taken it over for himself. It contained some of his treasures, including his iPod, laptop, a stack of rugby magazines, and various items of furniture and crockery begged or stolen from different sources. Pages from some long forgotten homework assignment were stuffed onto a shelf, and a battered tin was always kept full of biscuits supplied by Nana

Hetty. Tom possessed the only key to this haven, and entry was by invitation only.

The friends were sitting there, discussing the latest on the case of the dead animals, and how the police had reported no advance in their enquiries. Tom handed around crisps from a large family-sized pack, and Stuart was standing by a window, looking out across the valley. Half listening to the conversation which was going on behind him, he watched as a large crow lazily circled low over the hedges. Another crow joined the first, and then another, and Stuart continued to watch as they gathered to sit together on a nearby low stone wall.

"At least there have been no more animal deaths," he joined in, turning to the others.

"I just can't work it out," said Tom, once again topping up his handful of crisps. "No animal would ever do that to another – and I can't think that a human would. I can only think of devil worshippers or somebody like that. But then Dunchester isn't exactly the world's capital of evil. I'm starting to think like Stu with his horror stories."

Stuart turned back to the window, grinning. In the short time his attention had been elsewhere, the crows had been joined by maybe forty more birds of various types and sizes. As he watched, more and more came flocking to the wall. Soon it was covered completely with chattering birds, jostling for position. More came swooping down, gathering in the branches of nearby trees. He'd never seen so many birds flocking together, and he began to feel disturbed at the sight. What was happening?

"Tom, come and see this!"

Tom came to stand by him at the window.

"Just look at that lot. I've never seen so many birds together." His voice suddenly changed. "Look out – they're on the move!"

Led by the huge crows, and as if with one mind the flock took to the air, and gathered above in a dense, threatening cloud. Tom and Stuart could only watch as the mass swooped onto the caravan, most of the birds landing on the roof in a thick blanket, scratching and squawking angrily.

"What's happening – are they birds on the roof?" Kate called out anxiously.

The sharp claws of dozens of birds scraping on the roof above them sounded terrifying – what would happen if they could find a way to get inside the caravan?

Some time ago, Abi had realised that she hated being in crowded, enclosed places. She always tried to avoid being caught in the narrow school corridors when people were jostling their way to the next lesson, and she even felt a bit panicky inside a busy, packed shop. Now, she felt her breath quickening, and the rasping, scraping sound of the hordes of birds seemed to be inside her head. She imagined dozens of birds swooping and flapping in this tiny space, getting caught up in her hair and scraping her face with their cruel, sharp beaks and claws. She smothered a moan of fear with her hand.

"Look out!" yelled Stuart. "They're getting in!"

One or two birds had discovered a small hole in the back window, hidden behind a curtain. One bird forced itself inside, and flopped onto the floor. It was followed by two more, before Tom raced to the window, grabbed a cushion and forced it into the hole. The birds inside flew around angrily, screaming harshly and attacking their heads. Stuart picked up another cushion and was soon joined by Kate in frantically swatting at the birds, knocking them to the floor. The shrill sound of angry claws, beaks and screams filled the caravan. Abi sat on the sofa, curled up and feeling sick with fear.

Then, it was all over as quickly as it had begun. All at once, the noises on the roof stopped and there was a great flap of hundreds of wings as the birds took flight. Kate put her arms around Abi and tried to comfort her.

"I'm sorry," Abi gasped. "I lost it, I'm sorry, I was useless."

Kate stopped her. "Don't say that. It nearly got to me as well, it was scary, the sound of all those sharp little claws and scratchy beaks. I don't want to think about what would have happened if they'd all got inside."

******

As if in answer to some silent command, the huge gathering of birds rose and headed off in the direction of the village.

Old Mrs Parker was pegging out her sheets on the line in her garden when the throng of angry birds attacked her. She turned to run into the house, arms protecting her head. Her quick-witted daughter managed to drag her indoors before she was badly harmed.

******

The children of the village playgroup were having their mid-morning milk and biscuits in the recreation park, when they were suddenly surrounded by scores of infuriated, screaming birds. The adults with them shouted and waved bags and cardigans, quickly shepherding their charges into the nearby King's Head, where they cleaned their scratches and tried to calm their terror.

******

The bus, on its way from the village into Durham, ran straight into the flock, travelling along close to the road. Dozens of birds attacked the driver, through the open window of his cabin, forcing him to swerve into a ditch at the side of the road. As if satisfied with the panic and damage they had brought about, and as if in response to some silent order, the birds flew off, dispersing as they went. Five passengers and the bus driver were taken to hospital, suffering bruises, scratches and shock.

******

Nana Hetty came hurrying out of the farmhouse, anxious about the children in the caravan. She insisted that they came indoors, as they were bound to be shocked by what had happened.

"I've never known birds behave like that – never in my life," she muttered, as she busied herself making tea and bringing biscuits.

"Must be all that global warning," Tom smiled to himself. Everything that Nana couldn't explain, she put down to global warming, or "warning" as she called it.

Abi thought that if Grandad Bill looked like the typical farmer, Nana Hetty was the typical farmer's wife: plump, bustling and rosy cheeked. She poured her husband's tea into his big blue and white striped mug. Tom decided that he really could do with a sandwich to help him get over the shock he'd had. He also helped himself to a biscuit.

"But this is another strange thing, like all the other things that have happened lately – this unbearable hot weather, especially over the last few days – the dead animals, horrible dreams – just add this to the list."

Abi said nothing. She'd not told anyone about her horrible dream of burning. She caught Bill's eye as he poured milk into his tea, and she somehow knew that he too had dreamed. She decided to change the subject.

"I did some research about Jane Wake," she told Bill. "There's something I don't understand. Why did the people in the village turn against her so suddenly? And those men from Parliament – why were they here in any case?"

Bill nodded.

"I read about this years ago. I had the idea of writing a history of Dunchester but I never got round to doing it. I planned a chapter about the village in the seventeenth century and I did some research of my own, in the Record Office in Durham."

Abi sat forward on the edge of her seat.

"So what did you find out?"

Bill sipped his tea.

"Well, it's all part of the "big picture" of what was happening at that time," he began. "To really understand what happened to Jane, you have to know about things that were happening in other parts of England."

He began to tell them about what he had discovered.

Chapter Nine

THE DEATH OF A KING

"Right," Bill began. "You have to remember that in the seventeenth century, we had a civil war here in England between the King and his Parliament."

"The Cavaliers and the Roundheads," Tom interrupted. "I always fancied myself as a cavalier, they wore cooler clothes and had better hairstyles."

Stuart ignored this.

"Religion was a big reason for the argument – and Charles I lost, and he had his head cut off – I like the gory bits of history!"

Bill nodded.

"Well, eventually England came to be ruled over by Oliver Cromwell, who had fought against Charles. He called himself the Lord Protector and he was supported by the Puritans, a very strict religious group of people. He controlled Parliament and he and his supporters wanted to know what was happening all over the country – there was still a great deal of warmth for the Stuart family. The old King's son was living in exile in France and he was eager to take up his father's crown if he had the chance."

"He was called Charles, like his dad," remembered Stuart, keen to show off his historical knowledge.

Bill went on.

"The Puritans made themselves more and more unpopular. They tried to impose their beliefs and their rule in everything – how people should dress and behave, how they should worship – and they even banned Christmas Day one year, saying that you should spend the day in prayer and meditation, not in merrymaking. Cromwell became almost a dictator, and the ordinary people came to resent his strict rule. Some began to secretly plan for the return of young Prince Charles. It was rumoured that the Bishop of Durham himself was in touch with Charles, and plotting to bring him back to England. Oliver Cromwell must have heard these stories, so he sent a commission up from London to enquire into the loyalty of the people of the North."

"There were three men in the commission," guessed Abi. "And did they stay in Durham?"

Bill finished his tea.

"Yes. The Bishop must have been terrified that his plotting would be found out, and he'd be named and executed as a traitor. Now, this is only my interpretation of what happened next. I tried to read between the lines – there's a lot that the old documents don't say, and maybe some evidence was destroyed deliberately, but I think that the Bishop felt the need for a 'diversion' if you want to call it that. He needed something to give him time to cover up his tracks and hide what he'd been up to."

"So Jane became his diversion," Stuart had quickly seen the connection. "They threw her to the wolves – or to the commission."

"Maybe that's what happened. At that time, belief in witchcraft was strong, and anyone who was known as a healer – even anyone who lived alone – could be suspected of sorcery. People sincerely believed that the devil was always lying in wait, ready to steal their souls and make them his own. It was a different world then, not just a different time."

"But how come the people of Dunchester believed the stories about Jane so easily?" Kate asked. "She had been well respected for a long time before this."

"At the time, our local vicar was a man called John Main, and he was the Bishop's nephew – he'd possibly been given the post through the influence of his powerful relation. It would have been easy for the Bishop and his friends to work through him and to 'reveal' Jane as a witch. John Main had the reputation of being a very strong, persuasive speaker, and people would have been afraid to go against him because the Bishop was their landlord and could have had them evicted from their homes."

"Jane had some powerful enemies, and they didn't play fair," Tom said softly.

Bill nodded his agreement.

"The commission seemed to have jumped at the chance to try a suspected witch. Jane's chief accuser was – guess who?"

"John Main!" reckoned Kate. "I'm starting to hate that nasty rat!"

Bill finished his tea.

"John Main was backed up by his cronies, and of course he, the local vicar, was listened to and believed. And it worked out for the Bishop. The commission were kept busy here for a week in the summer of 1655, which gave Bishop Hood ample time to cover his tracks. Jane must have been shocked and horrified that her friends had turned against her, led by the vicar himself. Main probably believed that what he was doing was right, and that the return of the King was God's wish, as he hoped Charles would support the old ways and keep the Puritans in check. He would have kept his conscience clear with that thought."

There was silence as everyone thought about what they had heard. Kate knew that her Grandad often described history as a great puzzle, where one or two pieces added changed the picture completely. Although Bill had said that the story was simply his interpretation of the facts, and there was no solid evidence to back up his theory, Kate had the feeling that this is what had really happened in that long ago summer.

"I feel sorry for Jane," Stuart said as if to himself.

Hetty had been thinking hard, her mind busy following several lines of thought.

"Bill, I know you always talk about strange things happening in the valley. Is Jane a part of that, somehow?"

Bill considered carefully before speaking. "I don't think what happened to Jane was because of the valley, or any power here, but it's all part of the valley's past, part of its story."

"I don't know about your old ley lines or clever things that that," Hetty went on. "But I was born and raised in the village and folk have always spoken about unexplained things happening. You know, this must be the only place in England where the streets are empty on Hallow'een – no dressed up children or turnip lanterns. No trick or treats. People just stay in and lock their doors, as if they know the real dangers of that night."

"These ley lines – you've mentioned them before," Abi scented another mystery. "What are they?"

"A man called Alfred Watkins, back in the 1920s, often travelled over the countryside when he was young," Bill began. "He collected local legends and folklore and he formed the theory that many ancient monuments and historical sites are located in straight lines. He called these lines 'ley lines'. Churches, castles, holy wells, standing stones – he said they were all in a pattern. Some archaeologists today say it's nonsense, but some people have taken the findings of Alfred Watkins a bit further. They say that ancient men placed their monuments to link with each other, and with the natural features of the landscape in a great design. They claim that leys mark the places of some kind of earth force or energy, and some even believe that leys mark the paths that the dead are able to pass along from place to place. Now, we have quite a few leys in the valley, and they cross – you can trace them on a map. These crossing points are supposedly extremely powerful and the odd things that happen around here may be because of our ley lines. It's one solution, anyway."

Hetty broke in.

"And that, I think, is the end of today's history lesson," she laughed. "You'll give these bairns bad dreams."

******

As Abi approached the front door of the cottage, she found a small dog, shivering and shaking inside the porch.

"Hello, Bodger," she greeted him. "What's happened to you?"

The dog refused to come inside the house, and that was probably a good idea, she thought, as the cats would object to a canine guest.

Obediently, Bodger followed her to the shed, and lay down there. Abi brought him some water and some cat biscuits, which he ate hungrily. She was pleased that his trembling had stopped and when Christine came home, she took out an old blanket for him to lie on, and agreed that he should stay there until he wanted to return home.

Abi woke with a start – one second she was in a deep sleep, the next she was abruptly and totally awake. The red numbers of the bedside clock said 2.55, and she lay for a few minutes, wondering what had woken her so suddenly. It was a bright moonlit night, and she climbed out of bed and looked out of her window. The garden and the surrounding fields were bathed in a sharp silver glow, with the trees and hedges showing as soft, dark shadows.

Someone was standing in the centre of the lawn, a small slender figure, dressed in a long dark cloak, with a deep hood covering its head. As she watched, the figure held out slim, white arms to her, in a gesture of pleading or sorrow, Abi couldn't decide which it was. She was rooted to the spot, not able to move away, even if she had wanted to. She felt no fear, just a great overwhelming sadness and a strange sense of loss. She turned her head away to rub sudden tears from her eyes and when she looked back, the figure was gone.

Chapter Ten

A VISIT TO DURHAM

They had decided to spend the next day in Durham, looking at the sights and touring the shops. Abi felt excited at the idea of seeing the ancient and famous city. They caught a bus from the centre of the village, and from there, it was a straight road into Durham. The weather was still very hot, and all the bus windows had been opened, to catch the slightest breeze. Strangely, as they neared Durham, the weather became noticeably cooler.

From the start, Abi loved Durham: the steep cobbled streets leading up to the castle and cathedral, the quaint shops with old-fashioned windows and the more modern, with their smart displays, the throng of tourists clutching guidebooks and speaking different languages – everything fascinated her. Kate had told her about the great holy man, Saint Cuthbert, who had lived as a hermit on the Farne Islands. He had been buried there, and when the Danes invaded, the monks had fled with his body, searching for a safe place for the Saint's remains. They had prayed to God to help them, and they had been led at last to Durham, then a small settlement on the River Wear. Kate described how legend claimed that before reaching Durham, the monks had rested in a field above Dunchester. A well had sprung up where Saint Cuthbert's body had lain, and the meadow had carried the name "Holywell Field" ever since.

Now Cuthbert's remains rested at the heart of one of the most beautiful cathedrals in all England. Inside its cool space, they found the graves of Saint Cuthbert and Saint Bede, the first true historian of Britain.

"Wonder if he always checked his evidence," whispered Stuart.

Kate showed Abi the black line set into the floor. Cuthbert hadn't liked females much and so long ago, no woman could approach his tomb, and the line marked how near they were allowed to come.

They stood silently amid the soaring decorated pillars and gazed around them. Every time Kate came into the cathedral, she found herself wondering at the strong faith of its builders, devoting their lives to such a work of belief and worship.

She imagined how a medieval peasant would feel in such a place. It must have seemed like heaven itself compared to his own dark, cramped home.

They spent the rest of the morning checking out the music and video shops and Abi bought a pottery hen with a funny face for her mother. They walked by the river, and ate good pizzas in a tiny bistro where the tables overlooked a shady river walk. Abi looked up at the enormous towers of the cathedral, thinking that from here it looked more like a castle than a church. She was thoroughly enjoying her day.

In the early afternoon, they decided to catch the bus back to Dunchester. Tom pointed out a heavy, dark cloud as they approached the village. It looked as if they might be in for some welcome rain at last. The little bus clattered along the road, then shuddered to a sudden stop as they rounded a bend. In front of them was a car, stopped by a herd of cows which had started to cross the road. Good-natured comments and jokes came from the bus passengers and Kate wondered that there was no sign of a herdsman guiding the cattle.

Suddenly, as if hearing some silent voice, the cows turned and surrounded the small Micra, starting to push against it, rocking it wildly. Abi caught a glimpse of the frightened faces looking out of the back window. The car would be overturned in a matter of seconds, and the passengers on the bus suddenly realised the danger of the situation. All joking ended, and the driver jumped down from his cab, shouting and waving his arms. He was quickly joined by some of his passengers, and people from other cars which had stopped.

They all shouted and waved whatever they had in the cars – coats, cushions, umbrellas, but the cows ignored everything, continuing with their attack on the first car. One cow turned her attention to the bus, advancing upon it purposefully.

Abi had always loved the large, liquid eyes of cattle, and their gentle curiosity, but this was something different. The cow glared through the window, its eyes hard and cold, and somehow empty. It lowered its head, then turning sideways, began to push against the side of the bus, causing it to shudder and shake. Some of the passengers screamed, and another two animals came to join the first.

The people in the road increased their frantic efforts to chase off the beasts, car horns were blasted and some folk linked arms together, advancing in a line, yelling loudly at the hostile animals. The passengers on the bus had hurriedly begun to climb out, and then, suddenly, it came to an end. The cows stopped their pushing and set off calmly to complete their journey across the road. A man dashed in front of the herd and opened wide a double gate so that they could enter the field. Someone ran to the Micra, pulled open the door and helped out the terrified driver. Her two crying children were comforted and someone used their mobile to call an ambulance. In a few minutes, the bus and the rest of the vehicles were able to continue their journey.

"That was scary," Tom said. "I'd never have believed that cattle would just attack people like that. It's just not natural."

"Another unexplained mystery," muttered Abi to herself.

It was quite cold as they got off the bus at the stop in the village, and Abi found herself shivering. Kate stepped down first, looked around, then gaped.

"This is like a battlefield – what happened?"

The others joined her on the pavement and looked around, shocked. The front street was trashed – full of rubbish, litter bins overturned and ornamental flower tubs smashed to pieces. The remains of a child's buggy lay in the road, and a car had been pushed into the window of the post office.

An electric wheelchair lay on its side in the road, and a rack of newspapers and magazines had been knocked over, the torn and tattered contents covering the pavement and road. Shopkeepers were busy sweeping up the mess on the ground and stuffing it into large black refuse bags.

"You guys have missed all the excitement!" came a voice from behind them.

They turned to see Taz, Tom's best friend from school. Taz and his brother Jimi had their Indian names, but Taz had been Taz from the day Tom had met him at playgroup. Like Tom, he loved sport and he and Tom were alike in most other things.

"It happened about two hours ago, man – a herd of cows – I think they might have been from Young's farm – came wandering into the village. It was quite funny at first – they looked just like they were coming shopping, and people were having a good laugh at them. Then they seemed to change, in a second, and became really mad. No one could stop them. They knocked over everything in their way. Old Mr Henderson was pushed out of his wheelchair and a lady just managed to save her baby in the buggy. They came to the end of the street, then turned back again. People weren't laughing at them then, they were screaming and trying to get out of their way – it's not funny when you're in the path of dozens of great angry cows! Then they just calmed down and went off in the direction they'd come from."

"We saw the end of it all," Tom told him. "They were trying to push over cars, and then some turned on our bus. They looked really strange – not placid like they usually are. Then they just became quiet and normal and went off into a field."

"Biggest excitement we've had here in ages," Taz smiled, then his expression changed. "But not nice for people who couldn't get out of their way, I feel sorry for them. The ambulance took away Mr Henderson and some others."

Abi tried to imagine how it would feel if a crowd of huge, lumbering and hostile cattle came advancing towards you, and you weren't able to get out of the way. She shivered, and didn't know if it was because of the thought, or if it was the growing cold which made her do so.

Great drops of rain plopped onto the pavement, then Abi felt her bare arms stinging.

"Look – sleet!" yelled Taz, "Must be the end of the heat wave! I'll ring you, Tom!"

He hurried to his house across the road. He was right, the rain was turning to sharp sleet. By the time the shivering friends reached home, thick snow was falling.

Christine had a half day holiday, and had turned on the central heating as the weather had changed. She quickly ran a hot bath for Abi, and found a sweatshirt and cord jeans to replace her wet summer clothing. Helping her in the kitchen, Abi told her about the strange day, and how a lovely trip to Durham had ended in a nightmare.

Christine shook her head.

"I've never known cattle behave like that. They're never hostile or threatening, it's totally out of character. Something must have happened to make them kick off like that."

"There were the birds yesterday," Abi reminded her. "Something seems to be going wrong with nature."

"And this weird weather." Christine looked out of the window and across the valley. "That snow is coming down as thick and fast as if it was February. Maybe it's all due to global warming. People seem to be blaming that for everything now."

She told Abi that she'd checked that Bodger was comfortable in the shed, and taken him more food. He didn't seem to want to return home to Jonty yet, and was unwilling to come into the house where two cats ruled over things.

Christine had made a warming stew and the evening meal was pleasant and friendly. Abi felt that she'd grown closer to David and Christine over the past days. She fitted in here and felt a new confidence in herself. She'd met new people and got on well with them, never having to think what to say, or to worry that they wouldn't like her or think she was thick or boring. She really felt that she was moving on to a new part of her life.

As for David, he was pleased that the sulky, moody girl of a few days ago was changing as the barriers between them came down and they came to know each other better. It had been a good idea to have his daughter to stay!

At the end of the meal, Christine yawned widely.

"Excuse me! Goodness, I'm shattered! I must have an early night – I had a horrible dream last night. I was in a wood somewhere and all the trees were on fire. I couldn't get away – I was surrounded. I could actually hear the crackle of flames and could smell the burning branches. I struggled and struggled but I couldn't move. I woke up in a panic, trying to scream, but it came out as a croak. Couldn't get to sleep again after that."

She shuddered at the memory.

Abi said nothing but went to bed early.

Chapter Eleven

MORNING IN THE VILLAGE

Jonty Ginks opened his eyes as wide as he could, then blinked rapidly several times. He shook his head hard, rotated his shoulders, and stretched his neck. These actions usually cleared his brain after he'd enjoyed one or two extra pints at the King's Head, but totally failed to work this time. His head still felt cloudy and heavy, "fozzy" as his old dad would have said. Jonty was by now becoming used to the strange feelings inside his head. He knew that over a period of time the pressure gradually eased, allowing him to carry out the simple tasks he had been set – shopping in the village for the few food items he needed, cooking, cleaning – and looking after Jane Wake.

Then, just as he would feel strong enough to make his escape or to call for help, he'd feel her coming back into his head, the sly cloudy fingers of her thoughts seeping in. And then the pressure tightening around his skull like a metal band, until he could do no more than sit at the table with his head on his arm and try to bear the pain and sickness.

He looked at the woman sitting in an armchair by the fire she'd insisted he kept alight. She felt constantly cold, even in this exceptionally hot weather which had returned with the morning. Mind, he thought firmly, she looked well enough for someone who had been dead for the last three hundred and fifty years. She looked nothing like a ghost or a spirit – she was as solid and real as anyone he knew, small and slim – and pale, too, but most definitely alive.

She had developed a liking for hot, sweet tea, and Jonty winced as he added three heaped spoons of sugar into her drink. From what he could remember from school history lessons, both tea and sugar had been great luxuries when Jane had been alive in the seventeenth century, and she was obviously enjoying them to her fill now. Then there were the HobNob biscuits, which she'd eat a dozen at a time. The TV was another thing. Jane had been fascinated at the thought of seeing what was happening across the globe by way of the "Vision" as she called it. She watched Sky News throughout the day, and nothing else – no drama, or comedy or game shows.

Jonty wondered if their concepts and complicated speech patterns were difficult for her to understand. But she watched the coverage from the world's trouble spots with a passion – the bombings, killings, terrorist activity, evidence of global warming – and she glared accusingly at Jonty as if she held him personally responsible for all the ills of the world.

Jane rarely spoke to him in words, but easily communicated with him from her mind to his. Jonty wondered if she had found it hard to put her thoughts into modern day speech, and that it was easier for her to speak directly from mind to mind. She rarely seemed to feel the need for sleep, and Jonty heard her leave the house late at night, returning with strange herbs and roots which she hung to dry in his kitchen. Once, she brought back two large books with ancient leather bindings, and she had been reading her way through them. Jonty wondered where she had found them, and guessed that she had hidden them in some safe place before they had come for her, on one bright summer morning all those years ago.

He had to admit that her appetite was good, although she preferred plain foods such as soups, eggs and porridge. Her dress was simple, long, and of some grey stuff with a matching hooded cloak. Her clothing was always clean – to keep your clothes neat and clean must be a doddle after rising from the dead, Jonty guessed. Jane looked at him, and with a sigh, he got up from his chair and began to make a fresh pot of tea.

******

The village was waking up, getting ready for a new working day.

It turned out to be 'one of those days' for many. Clocks and watches stopped, and TV and radios were dead. Cookers refused to work and electric kettles stopped in mid-boil. Hot water suddenly cooled in the shower, hair dyers and tongs stayed cold, and toasters burned every slice of bread. Shavers gave their users nasty shocks and several cars took ages to start. The inhabitants of Dunchester began their day in a grumpy, bad tempered manner and then, as is often the case, found that their day became progressively worse.

******

Up on Crow Hill, Stuart took his coffee into the sitting room. He could hear his brother and sister shouting at each other upstairs. His parents were at work in the farm office, and he was looking forward to catching up with a sci-fi serial he'd been watching. He put his mug on the floor and scrolled through the programme guide. Finding the one he wanted, he selected the channel and groaned as the screen passed to its pale blue shade, with no hint of a picture. He tried the programme guide again. The screen remained blue, but a faint shape began to form in its centre, a dot which grew and darkened as he watched. He felt a faint unease as the dot began to shape itself into a figure. A figure dressed in a long cloak, its face hidden deep inside the hood. Stuart found that he was holding his breath in fear as the figure glided forwards into the screen, becoming clearer and closer all the time.

He felt that if he didn't do anything to stop it, she – somehow he sensed that the figure was female – was going to step out of the TV and directly into his sitting room. With a little cry, he zapped off the set and for good measure pulled its plug out from the socket. He heard Tom running downstairs and went to meet him, badly needing other human company. He found it impossible to tell anyone what had happened, and avoided turning on the TV after that.

Left to herself upstairs, Kate picked up a packet of photos which her mother had collected from the chemists for her. Kate had her sights set on a career in art, and she had been advised by her art teacher to begin to collect pieces of her work into a portfolio. Mr Hardy had also loaned her one of his classic cameras, with a roll of film to take sepia photographs. She had spent an enjoyable day finding interesting subjects, and she was looking forward to seeing the results. She had taken the first photo on the edge of the small copse at the foot of Maiden Hill, when the evening sun was low and mellow. She was pleased at the effect she had captured. The trees in the foreground were separate and distinct, their shadows falling darkly on the grass, and those further away melted together in a lacing effect of light and darkness.

"Cool," she whispered, then held the photo close.

There had been no one else there at the time she was working, she was certain about that – yet was that a figure in among the tree shadows?

It looked like a person standing there, wearing a long, old-fashioned cloak. For a second she wondered if it had been a ghost, but everyone knew that you couldn't photograph a ghost – even it they existed, which she doubted. But what – or who – had been standing there watching her? She flicked through the rest of the photographs, but there was no trace of any mysterious figure in any of them. Thoughtfully, she put the photos back in their packet and went to join the others.

Chapter Twelve

TOM THROWS A PARTY

Tom's birthday was on Monday, and he'd decided he'd like a proper grown-up family supper to celebrate, "with no kid's stuff".

"I suppose that means no birthday cake," said Liz, his mother calmly. "I'm glad I didn't bother with one, then."

Tom looked aggrieved. "Yes, I want a birthday cake. People who are a hundred have birthday cakes!"

Liz didn't tell him that she'd ordered his cake from a local baker a month ago.

Grandad Bill and Nana Hetty were invited, and Abi with David and Christine. Tom had opted for a Chinese meal, and a great many different dishes had been ordered from the takeaway in the village. Abi and Christine had gone shopping in Durham that afternoon and had bought him a snazzy rugby top. His presents were opened in record time. Once a mountain of wrapping paper was discarded, everyone moved to the kitchen to have the supper which had just been delivered.

The meal was a great success, with everyone talking and sampling the various foods at the same time. Afterwards, because it was such a lovely evening, the party moved outside, the grown-ups with their wine and beer, and cokes and juice for Tom and the others. A soft summer darkness was falling, and the first stars were appearing.

Alfie joined them, flopping onto the grass with a loud grunt, and from a distance came the faint call of some night creature. Kate glanced anxiously at the copse behind her, but there was no trace of any mysterious figure among the trees.

Abi sighed with contentment. This had been a really lovely evening, she thought – lots of friends together, lots of relaxed laughter, and a great meal. She realised that she was completely happy, and forgetful of the strange things which had happened lately. But that thought in itself brought back remembrance.

David was asking Young Bill if there's been any word from the police about the dead animals. Young Bill shook his head.

"Last I heard they were still carrying out tests – all they can tell is that all the animals had every drop of their blood drained."

Kate shivered.

Her father went on. "And still no one has any idea about what made the birds flock and attack as they did. I've spoken to farming friends in various places and they've never heard anything like it. It's a mystery."

"There was a horror movie like that – it was called *The Birds*," Stuart whispered to Abi. "The birds started to attack people for no reason. They pecked people's eyes out."

His mother heard him and threatened that he'd be banned from any more movies if he kept on like that.

David nodded to Christine. "There you go – another mystery for you. You're always keen to tell me all the strange things that are supposed to happen in the valley."

"Well, they do," Christine said firmly. "It's hard for you to understand, I know, with you being an 'outsider' as well as a scientist, but anyone who was born and brought up here, knows very well that weird things do happen."

David raised his glass to her in salute.

"Clocks stop now and then, and unusual things happen in nature, Chris. It's life."

"Christine's right," Liz broke in. "My old grandma lived in the village all her life, and she could tell you some tales. She knew the exact minute her husband died, even though his ship was in the middle of the Atlantic. She was preparing vegetables, looked up and there he was, standing there. Then he disappeared. She knew right away that he was dead. She checked the time and sure enough, when she was informed of his death, that had been when his ship had hit a mine."

"What about James Goodson who had the King's Head years ago," Hetty added. "He told me that he actually met himself coming downstairs – he saw himself as clear as could be. I remember thinking at the time that he wasn't long for this world, and sure enough, he was dead in a month."

"Dad's seen a ghost of a Roman soldier, haven't you?" Stuart asked.

Young Bill grinned and took a sip of his beer.

"One night I thought I did see a Roman, in full uniform, he looked distraught, searching in the bushes along the lane as if he'd lost something. It was either a ghost, or the effects of my night at the Young Farmers' Christmas party!"

Everyone laughed, and David turned to Old Bill, who had been quietly listening to all that was being said. "You'd put all this down to your ley lines, would you, Bill?"

"You can laugh, young man, and I don't claim that leys are to blame for everything that happens here, but it does make you think. All I can say is that you should keep an open mind. Some of the things that we know about today would have been regarded as impossible and far fetched a generation ago. We're learning all the time."

"So where are your leys here, then?" David looked about him. "Can we see anything of them? Any proof?"

"Just you look on a local map, you'll be able to see the leys, and you'll see that several of them cross in the valley. And supposedly, when leys cross, a sort of energy develops. I don't say that's true, but it's a theory, and we should consider all theories until they're proved wrong."

He pointed to Maiden Hill behind them.

"Now the old name for that hill is Maiden's Dance – possibly priestesses from some ancient religion met there. A ley starts there. Down the road there's Holywell field, where the monks rested with Saint Cuthbert's body before entering Durham. The line of the ley passes through, then hits St Michael's Church, then goes on to end at Durham Cathedral. Get you map out, David – just check it!"

David was enjoying himself, his scientific mind not at all convinced by what he was hearing.

"So thousands of years ago, men who couldn't read or write or even build in stone could recognise this incredible power in the earth? Bill, you tell a good story!"

From where she sat, Abi imagined these lines of power, meeting and crossing like glowing lines of silver across the valley.

Chapter Thirteen

ALL FALL DOWN

Next morning, the weather was as hot as ever. Everyone knew that English weather changed dramatically, but lately it had been ridiculous! Abi switched on the local news on TV, she thought the presenter was funny, with his dry humour and witty comments. This morning, his top news story was about Dunchester, and he listed the events of the past few days.

"Strange extreme weather conditions, dead sheep, ruined crops, birds attacking local inhabitants, and now marauding cows in the high street! It's no wonder the residents are calling Dunchester the Village of the Damned!" He smiled cheekily. "Of course, the village is said to be forever cursed by the local witch, Jane Wake – makes you wonder!"

Abi turned off the TV angrily.

"I've not heard anyone talking about the 'Village of the Damned'," she murmured, but the catalogue of all the weird happenings had only echoed her own thoughts.

Going into Christine's tiny study, she found a local OS map and a ruler. She took them outside and spread the map out on the garden table. She found she could easily follow the line Grandad Bill had identified. Maiden Hill – Holywell field – then the line crossed the village green, opposite the King's Head, before reaching St Michael's then ending at Durham Cathedral. Very strange. Old Bill had said that several ley lines crossed in the village – could she find any more?

Carefully, she studied the map. Across the valley lay the village of Ebchester. She remembered seeing a dictionary of place names on one of the book shelves and went to get it. She found that Ebchester was associated with the Saxon Saint Ebba and her church was in the village. Another ancient site, then. Her finger traced a route down the valley. Monkside Farm – could that have something to do with a monks' settlement there at one time? Old Bill had said that there had been strong links with the monks of Durham in the past, maybe they had built on the site of some ancient holy place. After the farm, the line continued through the old Roman fort, and then reached Dunchester, crossing the first ley opposite the King's Head.

"The place Jane Wake was burned," Abi said quietly to herself.

She followed the line of her ruler, and saw that the ley ended at Finchale Priory, on the banks of the river Wear outside Durham.

She felt that she lacked any further local knowledge which would allow her to identify any more leys, but she was confident enough in Grandad Bill's research to believe that there were indeed several ley lines crossing in the valley – or in Dunchester, to be exact. She gazed thoughtfully at the vista in front of her, and imagined a whole network of glistening leys, like a web, weaving across the countryside, and intersecting down in the village below her. Lines of power? Pathways for the dead? She sensed she was in for some kind of great discovery.

Abi felt it was time to have a long talk with the others, although she couldn't bring herself to tell them some of the things she had experienced. Those things were too private and personal to share. Yet there were too many unexplained things happening – they needed to sit down and exchange ideas.

She found the others in Tom's den, and decided to jump straight into the conversation, while she was feeling confident.

"Listen," she began. "I think we should talk, this is important. All of these strange things –"

She was interrupted by the funky tones of Tom's mobile.

"Soz, Abi," he apologised and spoke into the phone. "Hi Taz! What's up?" Faint noises came from the phone and Tom sat up from his lounging position. "What do you mean? Say that again. Taz? Taz?"

Quickly he called his friend back, then scowled at the mobile. "There's no answer – nothing."

"What's the matter?" Kate asked.

"Taz. He says his brother has the plague."

There was a stunned silence. Plague? Wasn't that a disease from centuries ago? Surely, it didn't exist now. Not in the twenty-first century. What was Tom talking about?

"He's joking," Stuart decided finally. "You know Taz – he'll do anything for a laugh. He'll be thinking this is hilarious. He'll ring back in a minute, you'll see."

"Wait," Abi said. "Tell us exactly what he said. Slow down and try to remember everything."

"Well, I answered the phone and he was, like, hyper – dead excited, worried. He said they wouldn't let him talk to anyone and they were taking Jimi away."

"Who's they?" Kate asked.

Tom shrugged.

"Dunno – someone who was there with him, I think. Then there were other voices, it sounded as if the phone was dropped – then nothing." He looked at the others. "I'm going to the village. I want to find out what's happening and if Taz and Jimi are all right."

Jimi, younger than Taz, was in the same tutor group as Stuart, always bright and full of fun. Stuart looked worried and upset, and of course, everyone wanted to go with Tom. They set off immediately and quickly reached the village by the footpath.

The Singhs' house was directly opposite the small Spar shop, and they knew the assistant, Connie, would be able to tell them anything that might have happened. Everyone called her the "Village Voice", a title she shared with the local free newspaper, and very little happened in Dunchester without Connie knowing about it and having an opinion to share.

She was busy serving a customer when they entered the shop, although there was more gossip than serving going on. Connie took no notice as they lingered behind the customer she was talking to.

"Well, they came for him about nine o'clock this morning. I got quite a shock – I mean I knew the little 'un was ill, a couple of days ago, his mum was saying he had a headache and a temperature. And she was really worried when she came in yesterday, said he had a rash and she was worried it might be meningitis. I mean, you have to be so careful with little 'uns, don't you? She was going to ask Doctor Ford to take a look at him. Next thing I know, they took Jimi away in an ambulance and the rest of the family went off in another. I only hope we hear some good news this afternoon."

They had heard all they needed to know and left the shop.

"The family were taken away as well?" Tom repeated. "And why in an ambulance? I don't like the sound of that."

He was obviously worried sick about his friend and his family.

"Connie said he had a rash," Kate said softly. "That would fit in with the symptoms of plague."

They sat down on two wooden benches, facing each other. They had all learned about the plague at school history lessons – that was one topic everyone knew about, and everyone remembered. It had been a truly awful time. The most frightening thing about plague was the speed in which it had spread around Europe, then around Britain at various times in the past. No one knew where it came from or how is was passed from person to person. Superstitious folk claimed it had been sent as a punishment from God because of mankind's wickedness. Not until centuries later had science discovered that plague had been spread by fleas living on the fur of rats, which had been so common that none suspected them as carriers of disease and death.

The first symptom was general tiredness and aching head and limbs. Then there appeared on the skin a rosy, circular rash, followed by great black buboes – swellings which could be as big as an egg. These gave the disease its name of Black Death. Most people died soon after, in great pain and suffering. A rhyme made up at the time of the sickness listed the course of pestilence:

Ring a ring o' Rosies ~

This described the rosy, circular rash which appeared on the plague victim's skin, as an early sign of the pestilence.

A pocketful of posies ~

The streets stank of sickness and death. It was believed that smelling this bad air could bring about the plague. Anyone going outside would carry a posy, made of herbs and flowers, and breathe through this, to try and cleanse the air they inhaled.

Atishoo, Atishoo ~

Some victims of the plague coughed and sneezed violently before dying.

We all fall down ~

This was the end for most of the unfortunate victims.

"This is all just mad – impossible. Plague was wiped out hundreds of years ago," Tom said, desperation in his voice.

"We don't know if this is plague, or something else." Kate was trying to calm him. "We'll just have to wait and see what happens. There's nothing we can do right now."

Some time ago, Abi's history class had been taken to Eyam, the plague village in Derbyshire. She remembered the sad story of how the plague had come to the village, and the inhabitants had decided to stay there, cutting their ties with the outside world so as to try to isolate the disease and keep it from spreading. She had thought at the time about how brave those people were, electing to keep the danger among themselves and not trying to escape. Many villagers had died, and their names were written outside their cottages, along with the date they had died.

Abi looked at the main street of Dunchester and imagined the same picture there. Would Dunchester become another such "plague village"?

They continued to sit there in silence, each of them occupied with their own thoughts, as around them the busy, purposeful bustle of the local shoppers talking, meeting and laughing went on. It was a strange feeling, to be part of this world and yet separate from it. A police car suddenly screamed past them and they watched it stop just before the road which branched off to Top Law. Another had stopped at the other end of the village, on the Durham Road. Two more descended from the minor valley roads, blue lights flashing.

"Must have been some accident." Abi guessed.

Stuart was deep in thought, then looked at the police cars as if he was seeing them for the first time.

"No – don't you see what's happening? The police are setting up roadblocks – they're cutting off the village. They think we've got plague here!"

As they watched, a white van drove up, and uniformed policemen got out and began to unload signs and barriers from it. Traffic was being stopped and diverted so as to bypass the village.

"Just four checkpoints will do it," Tom said, his voice cold and flat. "That would close the roads and block off the village totally. That will cut us off."

They were all too frightened and upset to stay and watch any more. They walked back up the hill in silence.

Chapter Fourteen

WHAT'S HAPPENING HERE?

Kate was worried. There had been all that stuff in the village and Tom hadn't said a single word since they'd reached home and flopped down in Tom's den. She knew her brother well, and knew that, under the shell of the self-confident, sometimes arrogant and mocking boy, there was a sensitive and caring person. Tom was desperately concerned about his friends, and he must have felt useless in not being able to help in any way. And the village was being isolated. That thought was really scary. All of them had decided not to say anything to the adults, until the situation became clear. Kate decided to start a conversation quickly, to try to take everyone's mind off their fears.

"Abi – you started to say something before..." her voice faded.

Abi nodded. "OK. Just let me finish before any of you say anything, and don't interrupt. Let me say what I need to."

She began by reminding them about all the strange events of the last few days.

"So nature seems to have gone mad," she ended. "Now, you've all said, or thought, that those were all unusual things – things you'd never heard of happening before this. Maybe something – or somebody – is making them happen."

Kate was staring at her – she must think I'm mad, Abi thought, but she was determined to go on.

"Try to remember. When did it all start?"

"It started when the animals were killed that day," answered Stuart promptly.

She shook her head.

"No – I think it began the day before that. The dead animals were a part of it, not the beginning. The day before, Frank pulled up the old tree and your grandad lost his temper. Just before he came storming up, the tree was pulled right out of the ground, and all its roots were in the air. I think – in fact, I'm almost certain that I saw something caught up in its roots."

"It was grey and oblong and it looked like a chest." Kate said softly. Everyone looked at her. "I saw it, just for a second, and then it slipped back into the ground with a whole lot of soil. Then Grandad came up, really angry, shouting and waving his stick. I forgot about it. When we came back to the tree, I had a quick look into the hole and there was nothing there. I s'pose I forgot all about it until now, when Abi reminded me about that day."

"Jonty had been there," Tom said, in a strained voice. "I can't remember him going up to the house with everyone else, and we all know how he's always on the lookout for anything of value."

"What I think is he'd seen the box or whatever it was, and he took it away in his jag when no one else was around," guessed Stuart. "I wonder what was in the box."

"The remains of Jane Wake, I think," Abi answered, in a quiet, unsteady voice. "There's an old custom that witches should be buried 'under wood and under stone' so that their spirit rests in peace; I read that. Well, there was definitely wood – the old tree – and the standing stone must have been there for centuries."

They all stared at her, each one thinking and trying to work things out in their head.

"So what are we saying?" asked Tom. "That Jane Wake has somehow come back to life and she's doing all these things? This is seriously weird."

"She did curse the whole village forever," Stuart was thinking aloud. "Now, if this was a sci-fi movie…"

"Don't go there, Stu! Don't even think about it!"

Kate threw a cushion at him to shut him up.

"I think we need to speak to your Grandad," Abi said. "If anyone can help us and give us some good advice, he can. I mean – I wonder if he ever suspected the remains of Jane were there. I can't imagine him not knowing something like that. Maybe that's why he was so angry that Frank had pulled up the tree and disturbed her." She paused. "There's another thing that no one's mentioned yet. A couple of nights ago, I had a horrible dream that I was burning. I suspect a lot of other people have had dreams like that." She looked at Tom. "Tom let slip he'd had a burning dream, and Christine has had one as well."

She had decided that some of her other experiences should remain secret; they were too close to her to share with the others.

"What's happening here?" whispered Kate.

Tom took it upon himself to act as spokesperson for the group.

"I don't know, but we have to try to make things right. I think we can all agree that there's something going on, and that everything points to Jane Wake – or her spirit, or ghost, whatever, being at the bottom of it. And I think yes, we should speak to Grandad for some good advice, but I think I should see what I can find out about Jonty first. He seems to have disappeared over the last few days, and that's not normal for him. And with Bodger turning up and not wanting to go home – maybe Jonty's ill, or maybe something's wrong. I'll go and have a quiet look around his place, see if I can come up with more information before we say anything."

Kate thought this was a good idea, as at least Tom could feel that he was doing something useful, and that could only be good for him. She nodded.

"Alright – but be careful, you don't know what might be happening up there."

Tom decided he'd go right away, and called for Alfie to come. Alfie wasn't a very fierce animal, but Tom felt the need of some company on his quest, and Alfie was always ready for a walk.

As they passed David and Christine's cottage, he saw Bodger at the gate and whistled for him to join him. He thought that neither dog would be of much help if there was any danger – Alfie would probably lick any enemy to death and Bodger would run away as fast as he could if anything bad happened.

Jonty's house looked empty from the road, but as they reached the gate, Bodger whimpered and lay down, head on paws.

He gave Tom an apologetic look, and Tom muttered, "OK boy, you stay here."

The curtains were drawn across the windows and both front and back doors were closed. That again was an unusual and ominous sign, as Jonty always kept open the back door leading into his kitchen.

Tom knocked loudly, listened, but there was no response. He tried again, then, holding his breath, he peered through the letterbox. All he could see was the kitchen table, cleared and tidy.

He listened again, and could hear nothing but the ticking of a wall clock. He called Jonty's name, but there was no answering call. As he stepped away from the door, his foot kicked against something. Looking down, he saw a stone box, similar to those sold in garden centres as planters, but like none he'd ever seen before. Skeletons danced around its sides, waving scythes and hour glasses, and Tom shuddered – they were the symbols of death, the stuff of nightmares, and he wondered where Jonty had found such a thing.

A stone slab which had obviously served as its lid was propped up against the wall, and Tom bit his lip as a suspicion came to mind. Was this the stone box the girls had described seeing caught up in the roots of the old tree? He felt that he didn't want to be there any more.

He called Alfie, who was sitting and watching from some distance away, plainly not wanting to come any nearer to the house. They set off for home, joined by Bodger.

"Lot of good you two are," Tom muttered. "Great soft lumps!"

He paused at the gate; he had the strange feeling that he was being watched from behind the closed curtains. He definitely didn't want to be there any longer.

When he got back to the others, he found that the police had rung his father, as with all other residents of the valley. Dunchester village was in quarantine for the next few days.

Young Bill was worried and baffled. Looking more and more like his father, he scratched his head. Nothing definite had been said, but he felt that bird flu was suspected in the village. All traffic in and out was stopped until the necessary medical tests were completed. Young Bill was trying to work out how he could manage without the farm workers who travelled from the village every day.

After hearing about Tom's call from Taz that morning, Grandad Bill and his son went into the office to discuss the situation, and to make some phone calls. But once again, they could learn nothing from the police.

"We can't say anything now about Jane Wake," Kate decided. "We can't spring any more nasty shocks on Grandad Bill. I think we should wait until tomorrow and then have a talk with him."

The others agreed. Tom slapped Stuart on the back.

"I never though I'd ever say this, Stu Pot, but for once in your life, you might have been right. Jane might well have taken the life force from those animals, to help her gain her strength. All those horror movies did come in useful!"

Abi was the only one not to smile at that. She felt that the valley was being battered by one horrible experience after another. Jane Wake had a lot to answer for.

Chapter Fifteen

THROUGH THE DARK OF THE NIGHT

Abi sipped her mug of tea as she gazed out of the kitchen window. It seemed that the weather was about to change yet again. Heavy clouds hung low over the valley, hiding the afternoon sun, and fingers of mist were twining down the hillsides.

That evening, both David and Christine were stopped on their way home from work. Only after they had convinced the police that they lived outside Dunchester, and must enter the village to reach home, were they allowed through the cordon. Both had been advised to stay home and away from work for the next few days, until the situation became clear. They talked about this at suppertime, comparing their experiences. They agreed that although nothing definite had been said by the police, it was hinted that bird flu had been discovered in the area, and scientific tests had to be carried out. First thing the next morning, they would have to ring their departments and explain that they had to stay away from work.

Then Abi added her news, shocking David and Christine when she told them that, in fact, plague might be present in Dunchester. Christine said she'd ring the hospital to ask about Jimi and went in search of the number. David doubted that she would be told anything.

"They seem to be keeping things to themselves: there was no mention about any of this on the local radio as I was driving home. They obviously don't want to cause a panic."

As Abi helped David clear away the remains of the salad, he glanced at the wall clock and frowned.

"That old clock's stopped – must need winding."

Then Christine appeared at the kitchen door.

"The phone's not working," she announced. "And I can't get anything on my mobile, just a crackling noise."

David had no better luck, and listening to his attempts to get through, Abi became aware that it had grown very dark outside. Looking out of the window, she could see nothing but a thick grey wall of mist around the house. Smoky tendrils of fog were brushing against the windows, blotting out everything from view. Then the lights went out.

Christine lit candles that she found in a kitchen drawer and decided that it was such a bad night that Bodger should come inside. She called his name from the kitchen door. He was not very keen to enter a house in which two cats ruled, but was glad to come in out of the cold and dank night. He slunk into the lounge, ears back, and lay down on a rug with a little grunt. The cats watched him from the chair they shared, but didn't take any action against him – after all, this was their house and he was only a guest. He knew his place.

Abi watched the fog curling and coiling outside, beyond the golden reflection of the candle in the window. It looked as if there were shadows moving deep within the greyness. Funny how your imagination worked when you felt isolated, cut off from the familiar world around you.

"It's going to be a long night," sighed Christine.

******

Down in the village, Helen Carson was sitting in her window, gazing across at the green, although nothing of it could be seen. Power cuts were frequent in Dunchester, although no one could ever give any explanation as to why that should be. She'd lit a candle and thought that she should feel quite cosy inside on such a horrible night, but she felt far from cosy. Fingers of mist writhed by her window, and sitting on a cushion on the chair he regarded as his own, Winston, her cat, looked at her through half closed eyes.

No, she thought to herself, "cosy" was definitely not the word she'd use to describe the evening. She thought that this must have been how it was hundreds of years ago: no electricity, no streetlights, no frozen foods. The village on its own, cut off from the outside world, enclosed within itself. Keeping itself to itself. Keeping its secrets. She'd been just about to settle down and enjoy her favourite *Coronation Street* curled up with a glass of red wine when the power cut came. Goodness, she thought, this is a bad night – supposed to be summer, too. She felt that her house was wrapped in a blanket, but then again, that was the wrong word to use. A blanket suggested something safe and comforting, and this mist was nothing like that.

The fog muffled all sights and sounds. The Spar shop had closed early, and the Chinese takeaway hadn't bothered to open at all that night. Mrs Carson tried to see if the King's Head was open, but strain her eyes as she might, she couldn't make out the big square building. She found she was worrying about her neighbours, and hoped Taz and his brother were well. She hadn't been able to get through to the hospital to enquire about them – the phone lines were obviously affected.

She gazed out at the street, past the flicker of her candle in the glass. She noticed idly that the fog wasn't really a solid grey wall, it was fluid, almost a live thing, constantly shifting and twining. Darker shadows came and went inside it, as if people were moving in its depths. Was it her imagination, or were there distant voices, murmuring, whispering? And that dull glow – was that a fire on the green? She desperately tried to make out the dim red light. Was that where all the mist people were heading? Winston's eyes flickered open and his ears pricked. She was suddenly glad that she had bolted her front door as the mist had settled. Helen Carson sensed that there was something very wrong about the village that night.

She remembered that a friend had recently returned from the Catholic shrine at Lourdes and brought her back a carved crucifix. She had questioned her religious beliefs years before, but she had thought the crucifix beautiful, simple and almost medieval in its dark plainness. She had placed it on the wall behind her, and obeying some deep need that she could not identify, she brought the cross from the wall and laid it by the candle in the window recess.

What was happening out there, in the midst of the fog? Yes, there were definitely voices, and a single scream from a woman, but she couldn't make out any words. The dull red glow brightened, and she could see sparks floating high into the sky.

From somewhere deep within herself, Helen Carson knew that this had all happened before. This was not simply another of those hideous dreams of fire and burning, but it had happened before. A great wrong had been done, and she had done nothing to stop it. She had spent the last thirty years as a teacher trying to explain to her children that if there is anything wrong, you must have the courage to speak out, to try to put things right, to stop people being hurt and frightened. Yet, once before, she had lacked the courage to speak out, and she must always carry the shame with her.

Helen remembered the words her old Nana had taught her. She'd said it was a very old prayer, told her by her own Nana. Funny that she thought of it now, after so many years. She closed her eyes and tried to recall how it went.

> "Through the long darkness of this night,
> please help us, oh Lord.
> Guard us from the shades and the shadows and bring us
> safely into the light of Your day."

Tears came to her eyes. Then, the fire glow was gone, the voices went silent and only the fog remained. Helen took a sip of her wine and thought about the past and its inheritance. Were we fated to make mistakes, and must we continue to learn the lessons of the past again and again? The past was a strange country. Could wrongdoing and weaknesses and mistakes echo through time until they were redeemed? Goodness, she thought, what strange thoughts. Winston watched her, unblinking.

******

Across the street, Connie Fletcher sat in her flat over the Spar shop. What an awful night this was! Not even the TV to keep her company and for her to complain about. She had locked up the shop when the power failed – no good waiting there with a candle, no one would venture out on a night like this, anyway. She worried about the food in her freezers – hope the failure wouldn't last long. Good thing everything was insured. She kept a close watch over the street – she didn't trust some of the local kids. Wouldn't put it past them to try and break in under cover of this fog. Well, they'd have to get past her, wouldn't they?

She took another sip of her sweet tea. Nasty thick fog – most unseasonable. You couldn't see what was going on outside. Anything could be happening and she'd miss out on it. She hated missing anything. Her great delight was to hear and pass on village gossip.

Connie craned her neck. There was something happening – shadows were moving in the mist and heading towards the green and the King's Head. She could hear the hum of voices and she could see the vague outlines of people. She switched on the torch she kept by her, and peered out of the window. That still didn't make the shapes any clearer. She must find out what all the movement and excitement was all about, or else she'd burst. She felt desperate that she was missing something. She pulled up the bottom part of her window and looked out. Tendrils of mist felt their way into her room, cold and damp.

The night was icy cold. The mist was thick and suffocating, and Connie felt herself fighting for breath. She felt that the very life was being drawn from her body and with a great effort she pulled her head inside and slammed the window shut. A glow appeared through the grey folds of fog – a bonfire on the green at this time of the year? She could hear distant voices talking loudly and eagerly. Connie took another drink from her tea, enjoying the excitement, but annoyed that she couldn't work out what was happening.

A shadow emerged from the mist in front of her window. It came nearer, and she could make out a slight figure dressed in a long cloak, the face hidden within a deep hood. Was this someone playing a trick, or dressed up for some fancy dress event?

She held her breath. She could hear a voice, but she was hearing the words inside her own head.

"Why did you betray me?" the words whispered insistently.

Connie gasped. What was this person taking about?

"I was your friend, I warned you about your careless tongue many times, but you wanted to boast that you had knowledge. You told them anything they wanted to hear, just to have their praise. I was your friend, but you betrayed me."

The figure slowly retreated back into the mist, leaving Connie with a strange feeling of loss.

******

Dan Rudd decided to close up the King's Head. He hadn't had one customer that night and he thought he might as well lock up and go upstairs to sit with his wife, Susan. Through the window, he saw an orange glow on the green, opposite the pub. The glow strengthened and he could see sparks tossed up into the night sky. He could make out shadows moving around the flames and could hear voices as from a very long way off.

Born and raised in the village, Dan had seen and heard many strange things. He had learned to keep his own council, and to keep well clear of things which had no direct concern to himself. So he ignored the temptation to go to investigate the patterns thrown onto the window by the red of the fire.

He slid the bolts into the door, blew out the candles, save one to light his way. He paused. He heard the faint, light steps of a woman passing along the corridor, and could sense the soft rustle of a cloak. He smiled and didn't turn around. It was only the little lass again.

Chapter Sixteen

A COUNCIL OF WAR

The fog had disappeared by morning, and the electricity supply had been regained during the night. Tom had found it difficult to sleep, there were so many confused thoughts going around in his head. Very early, he dressed and, in the quiet brightness of the new day, took the footpath to the village. Alfie followed, with slight detours into interesting bushes. They stayed out of sight of the police car at the nearest entry to the village. None of the shops looked as if they were prepared to open, with signs in their windows saying they would be closed until further notice.

Tom knew that the villagers, accustomed to often severe weather, were used to keeping a good supply of tinned and frozen food, so everyone would have enough to last for several days. At least there was no immediate danger of starvation.

He was shocked at the sight of three houses with large red crosses painted on their front doors. Tom knew that in the time of plague, if any member of a family showed signs of the sickness, the whole household had to be locked inside their home for forty days, in the hope that the pestilence could be contained there. Such houses had a red cross put on the door, with the words "Lord, have mercy on us" added. He had often imagined that horror – to see all your family dying in agony, locked away, with no hope of help and then you became ill yourself and died. He had heard that some people ignored the needs of their sick relatives, not daring to go near them, desperately trying to keep themselves safe. He shivered. Was someone playing a sick joke in painting these crosses? Or was it some ancient folk memory, and these houses had been marked as places of disease. He felt sick and didn't want to stay. He felt the village was dying.

When he reached home, he came across Grandad Bill, sitting outside and smoking a cigarette which Hetty had banned him from smoking indoors. Bill saw the strain on his face, but was too wise to comment.

"You're up and about early, lad," he said softly.

Tom nodded and sat down beside him. A long time passed in silence.

"Grandad, we need to talk," he said at last.

Bill nodded. "Aye, whenever you want, lad."

"Not now, everyone needs to be here. It's about all the stuff that's been happening."

Bill said nothing for a minute or two, then he said thoughtfully, "I've been tossing a few things around in my mind as well, Tom. I reckon it's time for us all to share what we know. You'd better invite everyone to a breakfast meeting, then. I'll let your Nan know."

As he'd guessed, this pleased Tom greatly, he loved Nan's big, tasty breakfasts. He suddenly felt better and grinned at Old Bill.

"Your mam and dad need to be told. And give Abi a ring – David and Christine need to be in on this as well."

Tom was glad to have something positive to do at last.

******

Abi had also had difficulty sleeping, and she too rose early, She had a lot to think about. By the time David and Christine came into the kitchen to make breakfast, she had decided that she had to tell them what had been going on – they really had to know. She asked them to sit down, she took a deep breath and launched into her account.

David, with his scientific background, found the whole idea laughable and incredible, and at first he believed this was some elaborate joke that Abi had come up with. Christine, aware of the strange qualities of the valley, was more prepared to have an open mind. David found it impossible to imagine that a suspected witch, burnt at the stake over three hundred years before, could somehow be "reactivated" as he described it, to work havoc in the area. He simply couldn't get his head around the idea, and he and Christine argued their views back and forth for a long time. They were interrupted by the shrill ringing of the phone. David answered it, and his voice was angry as he recognised the caller.

"Look Bill, just what nonsense have you been feeding my daughter?"

Christine motioned Abi to leave him and they took their mugs of tea into the lounge. David joined them later, looking thoughtful. He had agreed to attend Bill's meeting, and at least listen to what he had to say. He respected the older man and trusted his knowledge and good sense. He refused to say more.

******

An hour later, the big farmhouse kitchen was packed with people, and the table filled with good food. Hetty had been busy and, like any farmer's wife, she could magic up a feast in what seemed like minutes. Huge dishes of boiled and scrambled eggs lay next to piles of bacon and mountains of toast. Fat sausages, grilled tomatoes, and mushrooms spilled from large oval plates and homemade jams and marmalades gleamed from their glass bowls. Tom began to feel much better. Everyone was talking at once, and there was a party-like feel about the gathering. After the enormous breakfast and gallons of milk, tea and coffee had all been demolished, Old Bill sat back and cleared his throat.

"Now, I think we should make a start. I know that some of you will find this whole thing difficult to believe." He looked at David, who dropped his eyes. "But I ask you to please listen, keep an open mind and remember that even today, science can't give an answer to everything. There are countless things we just don't understand."

Slowly, David nodded.

As the oldest of the four friends, Kate elected to begin the story, going over the whole list of strange events of the past days – the freak weather conditions, the death of animals, the odd behaviour of birds and cattle, the nightmares about fire and burning, suspected cases of plague in the village, the horrific fog of the night before. Young Bill broke in.

"By the way, I rang the police yesterday and asked if they were any further on in the investigation into the illness in the village, but the answer told me nothing. It was all very bland and it sounded as if the officer was reading from a prepared statement. Tests ongoing but nothing positive yet, and the village was to remain in isolation for now."

Abi took up the story, describing how she and Kate thought they'd seen a stone box brought up by the digger when the old tree was uprooted. Tom chimed in then, saying he'd seen such a box outside Jonty's back door. He turned to Old Bill.

"Grandad, did you ever hear any rumours that the remains of Jane Wake might be buried on the farmland?"

Bill sighed. "She was said to be friendly with a farmer who lived here, and it has been claimed that they were buried somewhere on the hill "under wood and under stone" so that her spirit would rest peacefully. I don't have to remind you that the site matched that description exactly. I suspected her remains might be there – my old dad was insistent that the place should never be disturbed. That's why I hit the roof when I saw that tree come up."

He went on to tell the story of Jane, and the historical context of her trial and execution. At last, the story was up to date. No one spoke. Young Bill cleared his throat. "So what we're saying is that the spirit – the soul – call it what you will – of a so-called witch has been brought back to life by feeding on the blood and life force of those animals?"

Christine spoke. "It does seem far fetched, impossible even, but we have to admit that something very strange is going on. What other explanation is there? And there's some research which suggests that if someone suffers a very violent death, strong emotions are released that may be absorbed and preserved by the stones and the earth around them. Jane Wake cursed the village when she was dying – maybe the curse was somehow preserved. Bill claims that several ley lines cross at the place of her death – maybe they have an effect too. And local people do claim that the valley and the hills around are full of psychic activity."

Young Bill moved in his chair. "All these things that have happened lately – they don't make sense – they're not natural. I don't know what we're dealing with here, but it's something I've never met with before. Dad's always on about how strange things happen here – well, this is the strangest!"

His wife put her hand on his arm.

"Bill, you and I belong to this place. You don't need me to remind you of all the stories we've heard over the years – stories told by our own friends, sensible and reliable people, who have heard or seen all kinds of unexplained things. If Jane's come back, I for one wouldn't be surprised."

Grandad Bill looked around. David looked stunned, out of his depth.

"I think we all agree, then. Jane Wake – or her spirit – has somehow returned and she's punishing the village for the way she was treated."

"What can we do?" Tom asked. "The village is dying. She seems determined to make an end of everything."

Everyone suddenly began to talk themselves, full of excitement and concerns. Stuart and Tom thought up ways in which Jane could be trapped and captured, each one becoming more and more fantastic and impossible.

Abi sensed they were letting off steam, trying to relieve tension by their often silly suggestions.

"Why don't we just talk to her," she said quietly.

Grandad Bill nodded to her. "Go on, Abi."

Chapter Seventeen

INVITATION TO A WITCH

There was a lull in the conversation and Bill smiled in encouragement. "What do you want to say, Abi?"

"I was just thinking," she started slowly. "Jane had been born and raised in the village. She must have had a lot of friends there, and she did a lot of good things. She must have been well liked before the government inspectors arrived, she was settled and had a daughter. Jane must have been happy in this place. Maybe she needs us to tell her how much damage and fear and hurt she's causing." She paused. "Maybe she needs an apology."

"But how do we get to talk with her? How do we explain things to her?" Liz asked the question everyone was thinking. "How on earth do you get a witch to listen to you?"

"There's one place that a witch can't leave," Grandad Bill said slowly. "If a witch enters a church willingly, she can't leave without repenting. If we could get her into a church she'd have to stay and listen."

"Well then, that's easy," Tom said lightly. "We just invite Jane for a little chat in St Michael's – see what she says to that!"

Then David surprised them all.

"The old barn," he broke into the conversation. "Bill, you've said that was once a chapel. Is it still a holy place after so long?"

"I believe that once a place is consecrated, it stays so for always – I'd have to check with the vicar, but I think I'm right."

"Will Jane not recognise that it was a chapel, and stay well clear of it?" Young Bill asked. "When was it built, Dad? Before or after her time?"

"It was built after – about the 1800s," answered his father.

"So if we keep the outside the way it is now, and clean up the inside, she won't know until she gets inside and then it's too late." Stuart smiled at the others. "Easy!"

"I don't like the thought of tricking the little lass," Old Bill mused. "But I suppose it has to be done."

"We need a plan," said Kate firmly, and everyone started talking excitedly again. Now they felt they had a way forward, something definite to plan for. Points were listed quickly.

"The barn has to be cleaned from top to bottom."

"We must make sure it's still a consecrated building."

"It badly needs a coat of paint."

"We need to get loads of candles – there's no electricity there, remember."

"Lots of flowers, to make it look more like a church."

"We also need help and support," Old Bill said loudly and firmly. "We can't manage all this on our own. We need to get the vicar on our side first. And I think we have to get some of the villagers up here – those whose families have lived here for centuries and know about the place. They need to know what's happening, and we need their support. If everyone agrees to the plan, I'll begin ringing around. Today's Wednesday, so can we say we'll make sure everything will be ready for Friday evening? How does that sound?"

He looked around, and was pleased to see the nods of agreement.

"Just one tiny thing," Tom said. "We need to invite Jane to be there. Someone needs to ask her."

A look of horror appeared on Stuart's face. Despite all his love for spooky sci-fi movies, the thought of coming face to face with a long dead witch terrified him.

"Contacting her through Jonty seems to be the best way. I'll go if you want." Tom ignored his mother's expression of shock.

"I'll come with you."

Abi was never able to say why she volunteered to back up Tom. Abi deliberately avoided her father's eyes. This was something she felt she must do. Slowly, solemnly, Tom nodded at her. The meeting turned to practical points – who would be responsible for the various tasks?

Tom and Abi decided that they must set about their business right away. They went outside to plan their course of action.

******

Abi and Tom looked at each other. They stood on Jonty's doorstep. They'd not said a word to each other on the way there, and now here they were, scared, but ready to support each other in what they were about to do. Tom nodded down at the grey stone box, drawing Abi's attention to it. It was just as she'd remembered seeing it last, caught up in the roots of the old tree.

"Right," whispered Tom. "Here we go." He knocked loudly at the door. "Jonty. It's me, Tom."

Silence from within. Once again, he knocked.

"Jonty, I've something to say. Please come to the door, this is important."

Silence. It was as if the house was empty, but Abi sensed that someone was there, and was listening.

A strange feeling came over Abi. She felt she was no longer thinking for herself, not really aware of what she was doing. Something was guiding her, telling her what to do and say. She lifted up the flap of the letterbox.

"Master Jonty, we need to talk with Mistress Wake."

Tom looked at her, shocked.

Silence from inside the house. Then, at last, they heard footsteps coming slowly to the door. A pause – then it opened. Jonty Ginks stood in the open doorway, looking blankly at them. Tom gasped, and resisted the urge to ask him if he was all right. He obviously wasn't. he looked pale and drawn, his eyes dull and distant.

Once again, something apart from herself seemed to be telling Abi how to behave. She bobbed a quick, old-fashioned curtsey.

"Master Jonty, we need to tell Jane that the villagers know she's here, and they want to talk with her. They mean her no harm, and maybe she needs to talk with them, too. They will meet with her in the barn at Crow Hill Farm on Friday evening at six. That's the only place big enough for a meeting."

Jonty turned his head, as if listening to a distant voice. Slowly he nodded to them.

"Aye. She'll come."

Abi looked past him, into the kitchen. The curtains were drawn shut, and all she could make out was a shadow standing among other shadows. She bobbed her neat curtsey again and, taking Tom's arm for support, she and her friend retreated down the path. They reached the gate to the road and Tom stopped to look back.

"What made you say and do those things?" he wondered.

Abi shook her head.

"I don't know – I just felt I had to do it, that it was the right thing somehow. Something made me."

"Well, whatever it was, it worked. Let's go back and tell the others that so far, things are working out."

******

Old Bill had rung the vicar, telling him what he believed was happening. At first, Paul Rose was understandably incredulous, thinking that this was some huge joke. Gradually his manner changed as he began to put the pieces of Bill's story together in the context of the shocking events of the past days. He confirmed that the barn was still a consecrated place, and suitable for the planned meeting with Jane.

Bill answered his many questions as well and as fully as he was able, and at last, Paul agreed that impossible as it seemed, the spirit of Jane Wake appeared to have been awoken and come amongst them to exart her punishment on the village. He ended the conversation by promising to research any rites that existed to drive away a witch, or to take her powers away. He arranged to be at the farm on Friday afternoon before the other villagers would arrive. As he put the phone down, Bill bit his lip. Paul's voice had sounded stern and harsh, not at all like his usual tone. It was as if he wanted to punish Jane again, to demand revenge once more.

The rest of the phone calls he made were just as difficult. He called his oldest friends, people whose families had lived in the area for generations, people he knew well, and people he could trust. All of them listened carefully, most believing that this was some elaborate hoax, but then gradually reaching the same horrific conclusion. Dunchester was being haunted and punished by a long dead witch. They had known Old Bill all their lives, they respected and trusted him and every single person ended their conversation with promises of help and support, and an agreement to meet at the agreed time on Friday.

They all knew well the strangeness of the valley, and the mysterious forces which showed themselves from time to time.

At last, Bill sat back in his chair and gazed at the phone.

"That's about all we can do at the moment," he said softly to himself. "The people who need to know do know, they're all prepared to help us. The next bit is up to us."

Chapter Eighteen

BELL, BOOK AND CANDLE

Then came a whirlwind of planning and preparation. Abi felt that she was living in a different universe. There were so many ordinary, everyday things to do – cleaning up the old barn, helping Hetty sort out extra plates and cups and generally doing whatever she could to help out. Then, there was the knowledge that the village was still cut off from the outside world, and every phone call to the police asking for fresh news was greeted by the same smooth, non-committal answer that medical tests were being carried out and any change in the current situation would be passed on to them.

Calls to Durham Hospital about the Singh family were just as unsatisfactory, with the switchboard giving little information and refusing politely to confirm or deny whether other Dunchester inhabitants had been admitted.

Then, of course, in the back of her mind was the knowledge that soon they were to come face to face with a witch who had been put to death over three centuries ago.

Bill heard from his friends in the village that extra food supplies had been brought in by the police and, thankfully, there had been no more cases of suspected plague. There was a complete news black-out about the events, and some people had tried to ring the local TV station and newspaper, but had quickly realised that their calls were being censored, as now connection to anyone apart from the police was impossible.

It did seem that rumours were beginning to spread in the outside world, saying that something mysterious was happening in Dunchester. Hints and stories were beginning to appear in the local press, but the police obviously managed all news, and the main idea seemed to be that avian flu had been discovered in the valley and thus, the area was cordoned off for a few days.

The biggest task was the cleaning of the barn. Rubbish had accumulated there over the years. Everything had to be cleared. The floors were scrubbed, the walls painted white, and the windows were polished. Every candle that was possessed by the three families was brought out, and the children collected great armfuls of wild flowers and greenery to display in a dozen vases. When all was finished, Stuart stood by the door.

"It looks different," he said. "Really different. It looks like…"

"It looks like a church!" Abi finished.

******

Friday morning came, bright and sunny after a light mist burned away from the valley. The world looked calm and safe. It seemed that Jane had decided to call a truce over the last few days, and there had been no more nasty surprises or shocks.

Last minute tasks were completed, chairs were contributed from the three houses and carried into the barn, making it look even more like a chapel, a place of prayer. Then a table was taken in and covered with a white lace cloth, to become an altar, a focal point. The room smelled sweetly of wild flowers and Abi once again felt its quiet and peace.

In her kitchen, Hetty began laying out the food she had prepared. There was a gathering air of expectancy, and everyone felt excited and nervous about what the day would bring. Dozens of items of cutlery and glasses had been loaned and several bottles of her blackberry wine were brought from the cellar.

The vicar arrived early in the afternoon. True to his promise, he had researched some of the age-old prayers and rituals against the powers of witchcraft. He opened a large bag he was carrying, to reveal small glass bottles filled with holy water and salt, which he told them were necessary in the service. He brought out a small silver bell, an ancient leather-backed Bible, and a fat beeswax candle.

"Bell, book and candle," murmured Grandad Bill. "You seem all prepared for an exorcism, Paul."

"Well, isn't that what we're doing?" Paul asked.

Old Bill said nothing.

He and Paul Rose went off together to plan the format of the meeting that evening. Paul had found some ancient prayers, condemning Jane for her spiteful acts and ordering her to depart the village forever. Old Bill had rejected any official prayer of censure. He sensed that what would reach and touch Jane would be words directed straight to her: something simple, coming from the heart.

Then, in ones and twos, the invited guests began to arrive, slipping up the footpath behind the village to avoid the police blockades. They gathered in Hetty's kitchen and complimented her on the range of pies, sandwiches and pastries she'd managed to produce. As the kitchen filled, there was quite a festive atmosphere as friends and neighbours met and gossiped, for the moment free from the fears and dangers of the past days.

Abi recognised several faces – Mrs Carson and the lady from the Spar shop – she hadn't looked well when she arrived, but the company and the conversation seemed to cheer her up. There was Mr Rudd from the King's Head, and a tall dark woman who must be his wife. The vet was there, sharing a plate of sandwiches with Miss Harris, the waitress from the coffee shop. There were workers from the farm, along with their wives and families.

The level of conversation increased gradually and everyone appeared to be enjoying meeting and sharing gossip or a joke – something that they didn't do very often these days. Tom was, as always, greatly appreciative of Hetty's cooking, and was helping himself to yet another piece of quiche. Grandad Bill felt that it was time to remind the gathering why they were all there. As Hetty and Liz filled up cups of tea and coffee, he stood at the head of the long farmhouse table and knocked a serving spoon on the tabletop. He cleared his throat and everyone stopped talking to look at him expectantly.

He began by thanking everyone for coming together, and for trusting him by listening to his request for their support. He reminded them that they came from the most ancient families in the village, and that they were all aware that Dunchester and its valley was full of unexplained powers. No one was able to say what these powers were, or to explain their source, but this indeed was a place that was "different". They all knew old family stories, which confirmed that the village and its valley possessed characteristics not found elsewhere.

Speaking clearly and thoughtfully in the hushed atmosphere, he pulled all the strands of Jane's story together, and linked it with the finding of her remains in the field, "under wood and under stone". He listed all the weird events which they had all experienced over the last few days. Unbelievable as it seemed, he concluded, it appeared that the ghost, or spirit, or some essence of life belonging to Jane Wake was now amongst them. He finished speaking and there was silence.

Old Bill cleared his throat and went on.

"I've no idea what we'll see tonight, or what will happen. Anyone who feels that this will be too much to ask from them can leave now, and they'll be no less thought of."

He paused, but there was no movement among the company.

"We must all stick together and support one another. Leave it to the vicar and me to do the talking. Remember, we'll be in a holy, consecrated place. Nothing can hurt us there, as scary as it may get. Just be strong for each other. We're not here to punish Jane. As I told you, there was a great wrong done to her. We just want to talk with her and try to put things right at long last."

An old gentleman stood up, erect and distinguished looking. This was Dr Dallow, who had brought most of the group into the world, and had been tending to their ailments ever since.

"Bill, this is an incredible story, and in other any other place, I'd have had you carted off for a medical examination." He stopped to let a ripple of soft laughter die away, then looked around him. "But we do know things are different here – ley lines, earth magic, call it what you will. I've known you all my life, Bill Oaken, and you're one of the most honest, upstanding men I know. I think I can speak for everyone here – we'll do as you advise us, Bill, we believe what you tell us and if we can right the wrong done to Jane Wake and let her rest easy, I say we should do that."

There was a shuffling of feet, and many sounds of agreement. Abi realised that she hadn't moved for a long time, and stood up to stretch. People around her were murmuring together and moving in their seats. The spell had been broken. Now it was time.

They all filed out to the barn and took their seats. Young Bill lit the host of candles and they flickered bravely in the first shadows of evening.

"Don't they look much like an army going to fight against the powers of evil," whispered Stuart. "Now, if this was a movie, they'd all carry torches and pitchforks. These are all just ordinary people – people we've known all our lives. They look terrified."

"I think they look wonderful," Kate said softly. "They might be terrified, but they're here to do what they think is right. I think that's what real bravery is."

Ancient lore says that the spirit of a witch can be put to rest with bell, book and candle.

Chapter Nineteen

OUT OF TIME

Inside the old chapel, the silence was broken only by a scrape of a chair, someone clearing their throat, or coughing. The smell of candles blended with the heady aroma of flowers, and Abi began to feel drowsy. Grandad Bill had placed himself just inside the barely open door, so that he could see any movement along the track.

"They're coming," he said suddenly. "Jonty and Jane."

Abi now understood the phrase "you could hear a pin drop". It seemed as if everyone had breathed in and forgotten to breathe out again. Grandad Bill remained by the door, while Paul Rose came to stand at the makeshift altar at the front of the room. There came two loud knocks on the wooden door. Bill opened it wide then stepped aside. A slight figure entered, dressed in a dark woollen cloak, its hood raised. Behind her stood Jonty, looking lost and absent from what was going on but, at the same time, obviously at the service of Jane.

It was only when the cloaked figure was across the step that the realisation came that this was actually a church. The figure stopped in its tracks, stepping back slightly as if about to retreat. Old Bill came forward and offered his arm.

"Welcome Jane," he said, as if thanking a friend for coming on a visit. "We mean no harm to you, lass, I promise."

His arm was still extended to the figure, and slowly a white hand came from under the cloak and rested on his. The figure drew a deep breath, and the two, as if following the steps of some stately dance came to stand at the front of the gathering.

A high-backed chair had been placed in the sight of the assembly. Bill escorted her there, as proudly and respectfully as if he had been a king and his partner a princess. Jonty followed her every step. Bill gave a courtly bow as he indicated where she should sit. She bowed her head in return, and sitting, slipped off her hood.

Kate had no idea what she expected to see. After all, this was a woman who had supposedly been dead for over three hundred and fifty years – what horrors would be shown when the hood was removed? Yet the face revealed was that of a young healthy woman, maybe in her late twenties, alive, attractive, and with a fresh, rosy complexion, her thick brown hair piled neatly high on her head. The gathering shuffled their feet and muttered together in surprise.

Jane looked about her, hands grasping the wooden arms of her chair. She spoke, and again, there was a shock. Some of those present had thought that her words would be difficult to understand – if she could speak at all. Perhaps her language would be old-fashioned, archaic. Yet she spoke as one of themselves, in a soft local accent, in plain, everyday speech. She gazed at the people sitting in front of her.

"So many faces that I know." Although she smiled, it was a stiff, chilling expression. "Why, there's Meg Fisher," she nodded towards Helen Carson. "Are you still chasing the bairns away from your hens? And Janna Brown! Have you still your poisonous tongue when talking about your neighbours?"

Connie reddened and looked down at her feet. Jane nodded to Dan Rudd. "Master Wilson, it's good to see you again. You were kind to me in those last days."

Dan bowed his head in silent salute.

Kate suddenly realised that she was hearing Jane's words within her mind. Jane was communicating through thoughts, not words.

Old Bill had come to stand next to her chair, and she looked up at him.

"And you, Farmer, you were always a good man, someone to be trusted."

Her eyes fell on Abi. There was no comment, just a long searching look.

Tom pulled at Kate's sleeve.

"She thinks we're the same people who lived here before – when she was here," he whispered, incredulous.

The same thought was clearly in Bill's mind also.

"Jane that was all a long time ago. These people are the children of the children of those you knew."

Jane held up her hand.

"No, Farmer, how do you know that we have not all been brought here again, for some purpose? And that purpose may be to give me justice – and revenge for what this village did to me."

She gripped the arms of her chair in a sudden surge of anger. Her voice was raised, and her cheeks flushed with emotion.

Bill stood his ground, calm and unafraid.

"Then, if we have been brought together again, the purpose may be to bring justice by giving us a second chance."

Jane was silent, regarding him with her great brown eyes.

"Jane, you belong to this village, you were born and raised here," he began.

She turned her head away abruptly, as if losing patience with him.

Bill persisted.

"Listen to me. We all know the good you did here – how many people you helped, how you gave advice about crops and beasts. We know how you looked after the health of your neighbours, and how you nursed their bairns."

Jane held her head high.

"Then they said I was a witch and served the devil. None would speak for me, everyone I called a friend closed their doors to me."

Her voice echoed through the silent chapel, lonely and hopeless.

One or two of the group looked distressed and cleared their throats. Then Bill told Jane the full story of the plot in which she had been an unknowing pawn – a story she had not known until now. She listened in silence. Kate could not read her expression.

"Jane, throughout history, the little ordinary people get caught up in the actions of the great ones and they suffer. You were just one little person who was sacrificed so that political events could take their course."

Bill spread out his hands in a pleading gesture.

Jane's fury had calmed somewhat, as she considered what had happened. She glared at the vicar standing at her other side.

"John Main." Her voice was thick with disgust. "I always felt you knew more than you ever said. You had high born friends – why, your uncle was the Bishop. You and I always argued about the real meaning of religion – did you hate me so much that you gave me to the fire?"

Paul Rose came to face her.

"Maybe I believed that I acted for the best of reasons – for my country and for my faith. Those Puritans in London would have put an end to our religion and imposed their own, if we gave them an excuse to do so. Perhaps I felt that by giving up one person I could protect many more, and I could even save our church."

There was a stunned silence. They had all noticed the words he used – Paul was talking as if he had been the vicar who had betrayed Jane. He even looked different, his young, fresh face taking on lines of care and conscience. Jane sat, still as a statue, staring before her.

Bill spoke once more.

"That's something that can be argued about forever, the price of a human life. But we have to move on. Justice was not given to Jane all those years ago, no matter what reasons may be offered." Heads were nodded all around the room. "But Jane, you mustn't hurt us any more. There must be peace between us. The village – your village – is dying. We understand that in your hurt and anger you wanted revenge, but too many things have been hidden. It's time for the truth, I give you solemn word that your story will be told, and that your good name will be honoured in the future.

The figure sitting in the wooden chair slowly inclined her head. "Indeed, enough has been done here. This is not my time, and I have no desire to stay. The world has not improved in the last centuries. Master Ginks has a magic box whereby you can see what is happening all over the world. There is so much cruelty and suffering – and done in the name of religion. You have not come far. As you say, I am out of my own time and have little love for this one. I have no other time, Farmer – there is nowhere for me to go."

It was Paul Rose who stepped forward, holding out his hand to Jane.

"Lady, we are all to blame for causing you distress and pain, and for robbing you of your good name. What happened in the past has had terrible repercussions throughout time. We apologise for our actions. The true story of Jane Wake will be heard in the future."

For what seemed a very long time, the two looked at each other, and it seemed that some great peace had been made.

The young vicar had carefully researched the ancient rites and prayers which dealt with exorcisms and the defeat of evil, but he now realised that what he had prepared was not enough; something else was needed. Jane nodded to him, as if giving him her permission to go on. He began to say the Lord's Prayer, joined by the congregation. Jane's lips moved soundlessly with them. At the end, he stood in front of the altar, and rang the little silver bell he'd placed there. He closed the heavy Bible and blew out the church candle he'd brought.

"I bless you, our sister Jane Wake, and set your soul free, by bell, book and candle."

Abi became aware of music approaching, sweeter than any she'd ever heard, and coming from a long way off. A quick look around told her that others were now also aware of it. The vicar paused in his work, the music came closer still, and the door of the chapel flew open. No one could ever forget what they were now seeing. There entered a large company of folk dressed in the rich colours and fabrics of long ago. First came a dozen or so boys, laughing and playing strange instruments – small hand drums and what looked like some sort of recorders.

They were followed by lords and ladies, smiling and talking together as if this were some sort of enjoyable social occasion.

Abi looked at Grandad Bill, wonderingly. He was smiling.

"These are the people of the village, come to take her back to her own times," he said softly.

Although the sounds of music and lively conversation appeared solid and real, the figures of the brightly clothed crowd seemed to shimmer and quiver, as if seen through a heat haze rising from the earth on a hot summer day. A man and woman reached out to Jane, smiling a welcome as they raised her from her chair. Every member of the ghostly gathering ignored the others present within the chapel, as if they were the reality and the others merely shadows. Jane was surrounded by the welcoming, excited group. The music now changed, from the bright dancing tune which had introduced them from somewhere outside. Now, the melody was softer, more stately, the notes rising in a sad, yearning harmony.

The company turned to the door once again, led by the group of boys playing their ancient instruments. With Jane in their midst, they made their way to the door, never halting or hesitating in their passage. The villagers remained where they sat, until the last sweet notes had died away in the darkening evening.

Later, as they emerged into the night, saying their soft farewells, Abi glanced up to Maiden Hill. In the shadows, cast by the ancient trees on its summit, stood a strange, small man, dressed in animal skins. He raised high the spear he was carrying as if in salute. Old Bill had fallen back to stand with her, and he raised a hand to return the greeting.

"Everything as it should be," he said gently. "Everything is right again."

Chapter Twenty
THE END?

The village quickly returned to normality. The summer weather was of the usual unpredictable sort and the birds and animals acted entirely as they should. All traces of plague disappeared and Taz and his family returned from the hospital laden with cards and gifts from well wishers. Jonty had no memory at all of his time with Jane, and returned to his search for "something special". No one who had been in the chapel that night ever spoke about their experience: it was too strange and mysterious to ever mention. But among their number, there would be the odd secret nod and smile, and a firm companionship which would bind them together forever.

Abi went home to her mother and Buster, and prepared for a new term. She felt different – she'd learned a lot about herself, and made some good friends. She'd faced danger and discovered something of the secrets and the magic of the past. She felt a new confidence in herself, and she knew that the friendships she'd made in the valley would stay with her forever.

Bill kept his word. As a governor of the village school he worked with Helen Carson to review the curriculum, so that the story of Jane Wake was investigated and studied by all students. He completed his book about Dunchester, and it was hailed as a triumph of detective work, with the research of Jane Wake described as a sensitive recreation of a past tragedy. He led a fund raising campaign to erect a small and beautiful statue on the village green opposite the King's Head. It showed a slim woman, dressed in a long cloak, her hood thrown back and reaching both arms high in a gesture of hope and forgiveness.